The Illustrated History of Gymnastics

John Goodbody

Stanley Paul

London Melbourne Sydney Auckland Johannesburg

Also by John Goodbody:

The Manual of Weight-Training (with George Kirkley)
The Japanese Fighting Arts
The Olympics 1972 (with Jim Coote)
The Book of Football
Judo – How to Become a Champion
Olympic Report 1976 (with Jim Coote)

796.41
600

Stanley Paul & Co. Ltd

An imprint of the Hutchinson Publishing Group
17–21 Conway Street, London W1P 6JD

Hutchinson Group (Australia) Pty Ltd
30–32 Cremorne Street, Richmond South, Victoria 3121
PO Box 151, Broadway, New South Wales 2007

Hutchinson Group (NZ) Ltd
32–34 View Road, PO Box 40–086, Glenfield, Auckland 10

Hutchinson Group (SA) (Pty) Ltd
PO Box 337, Bergvlei 2012, South Africa

First published 1982
© John Goodbody, 1982

Set in Plantin 11 on 12 point by Imago Publishing
Printed in Great Britain by The Anchor Press Ltd
and bound by Wm Brendan & Son Ltd,
both of Tiptree, Essex

British Library Cataloguing in Publication Data
Goodbody, John
  The illustrated history of gymnastics.
  1. Gymnastics – History
  I. Title
  796.4'1   GV461

ISBN 0 09 143350 9

Frontispiece: *Olga Korbut displays her extraordinary flexibility*

'I have seen old photographs that show
women's gymnastics forty years ago. A lot
of people laugh about it now; it all seems
very primitive and childish to them but
it shouldn't be laughed at. What I do now
will surely be surpassed one day.'

Vera Caslavska

For Jim Coote, who died

Contents

Foreword

by Nik Stuart, Director of Technical Development at the British Amateur Gymnastics Association

With careful, sympathetic research John Goodbody has produced a milestone in gymnastics literature – I am most grateful to him, for I was totally absorbed reliving the events he describes so accurately.

John Goodbody's book is an engagingly frank, factual, graphic story of the sport and its heroes and heroines, giving the joys and tragedies of the years an evergreen impact. Linked with so many beautiful and evocative photographs, the author's text tells the story in such an enthusiastic and infectious way that I read it from start to finish in one sitting. I almost expected Tourischeva to dance out of the covers, such was the effect the book had on me, and it's all true for in most cases, 'I was there!'

Gymnastics is lucky to have found such an exceptional crusader for our sport. Thank you, John Goodbody.

Introduction
and Acknowledgements

It is curious that no history of so popular and enchanting a sport as gymnastics has previously been written. This book is intended to fill the gap. The sport has particularly flourished over the last ten years but it has enjoyed a long competitive history, being part of the initial modern Olympics in 1896 and staging its first world championships in 1903 far earlier than most major sports.

Although movements were, for many years, rudimentary and the interest restricted, gymnastics was gradually provided with a framework and organization for its sudden popularity in the 1970s. Now its leading female performers are as fêted as film stars.

I would like to acknowledge the help given to me in writing this book by many institutions. These include the British Olympic Association; *The Sunday Times*; United Newspapers, former publishers of *World Sports*; the Physical Education Association of Great Britain and Northern Ireland; Leeds Polytechnic and Carnegie College; and *L'Equipe*, the French daily sports newspaper.

The British Amateur Gymnastics Association and *The Gymnast* also provided much background information. Alan Burrows, Nik Stuart, and Jim and Pauline Prestidge have always guided my enthusiasm towards the right channels in the sport. Teresa McLean was invaluable for details of the Middle Ages. Sarah Windebank typed the manuscript and Marion Paull was a painstaking editor.

John Goodbody
Paris, April 1982

The ancient Olympics : a winner enters
the Temple of Zeus (from a drawing
by A. Castaigne)

1 The Early Days (to 1896)

Olympic gymnastics has had a long, chequered and curious history. Usually encouraged, but sometimes opposed by physical education authorities, it has been ignored by the general public until recent years, when the popularity of the women's sport has been overwhelming, its competitors becoming as celebrated as leading film stars. The men's sport, however, has yet to generate equivalent enthusiasm, something unique among Olympic sports where male performances arouse most interest.

The Greeks wouldn't have approved of this trend. For sport in most parts of Ancient Greece was for men, and women were often barred from the stadiums and training places, even as spectators, perhaps partly because men often took part unclothed. The word 'gymnastics' derives from the Greek *gymnos* (naked), and 'gymnasium' originally meant a public place or building where Greek youths exercised. Although many ancient civilizations, including the Chinese, Persians and Indians, followed a strict code of exercises, it was the Greeks who laid emphasis on physical training and promoted the ancient Olympic Games.

Even before the first Games (776 BC), gymnastics had been celebrated on Crete during the Minoan civilization (2700–1400 BC). The Knossos frescoes depict acrobats leaping over the horns of a bull, symbol of primordial male power and honoured as the root of all life and fecundity. There are records, too, of the king's acrobat vaulting a vertical sword.

Despite the evident early interest in gymnastics, the sport, as we know it, was never part of the ancient Games. The Greeks had not invented the system of competition scoring and apparatus with which we are familiar today. Rather, it was regarded as training for other sports, particularly athletics and wrestling, two principal events of the ancient Games, and also as a means of physical exercise. The state-built gymnasiums, almost an ancient equivalent of the modern-day leisure centre, included areas for academic instruction and art, as well as sport. The gymnasiums have become famous for the schools of philosophy which originated there: Plato held discussions at the Academy and Aristotle at the Lyceum.

When the Roman Empire succeeded the Greeks, gymnastics began to be used for military training. Among the apparatus the Romans introduced was the wooden horse. Mounting and dismounting were military skills and the cavalry needed to be proficient at them. In AD 393 the Roman Emperor Theodosius abolished the ancient Olympic Games, which had become increasingly professional and then corrupt. This was one cause of the decline of many sports, including gymnastics. Another was the spread of Christianity. The rigorous medieval belief that the body housed Satan led inevitably to a reduction of interest in any activity that celebrated or increased its powers.

By the time the Games were finally revived in 1896, gymnastics had enjoyed a recovery. The reawakened interest in education following the Renaissance affected not only academic but also physical exercise. Gymnastic movements had been perpetuated by troupes of entertainers, similar to modern-day circuses. Rabelais, the sixteenth-century French writer, records the popularity of wandering acrobats, who used to erect a bar or rope between two trees 'and there did swing by the hands touching at nothing'.

During the Middle Ages gymnastics had formed part of minstrelsy, which had two main features. The first was the singing and telling of stories, usually accompanied by the harp or pipe. The other was tumbling and leaping by 'mimi', mime artists, also called 'scurrae' (scurrilous artists or bawds), whose morality was clearly questionable. The mimi worked in travelling troupes, going from household to household, from halls to village greens.

Women were popular gymnastic dancers and their movements were performed to music, like the modern floor exercises. One famous woman was Matilda Makejoy, who was in and out of royal service for fourteen years. She performed in 1306 when England's King Edward I celebrated the knighting of his son with a feast for 300 nobles. Balancing – and again the associations with modern gymnastics are evident – was popular in the fourteenth century, partly because noblemen returning from the court of Frederick II of Sicily admired the deft performances of Saracen girls and so similar exhibitions became popular in England. A fourteenth-century routine consisted of cavorting on the edge of a tambourine as it rolled jingling along the floor. One Venetian dancer was paid £16 13s. 4d. by Richard II in 1380. Children's gymnastics was also admired; thus the daughter of John Brandon, one of King Henry VIII's jugglers, did 8d. worth of tumbling to entertain the Prior of Worcester in 1519. Olga Korbut certainly had her predecessors.

Activity was not confined to England. One of the most spectacular and popular medieval tales is the French thirteenth-century story titled *The Tumbler of Our Lady*, which records how a former minstrel retired into a monastery in Clairvaux, Burgundy. The austerity of the Cistercian monastery unsettled him and he wasn't well-enough spoken to join in the singing of service. The tale records: 'He had lived only to tumble, to turn somersaults, to spring and to dance, to leap and to jump. This he knew but naught else.' So he had to go down to the crypt to worship Our Lady in the only way he knew. As the mass bell rang, he used to take off his habit and begin exercising. He continued until he 'was covered with sweat as the grease issues from spitted meat'. He was overcome by the heat and collapsed, but was revived by an angel sent by Our Lady. The other monks, suspicious of his frequent absences, spied on the tumbler and reported the incident to the Abbot, who decided he was under Our Lady's special protection. Tumblers were subsequently considered especially blessed.

During and after the Renaissance, writers also began to stress the importance of physical development. The French essayist Montaigne recommended exercise in *Of the Education of Children,* and Frenchman Jean-Jacques Rousseau in *Emile* and British philosopher John Locke in *Thoughts Concerning Education* were equally enthusiastic about physical training for the young man. Rousseau writes: 'Exercise his body continually; make him strong and healthy that you may make him wise and reasonable.'

The Swiss educationist Johann Heinrich Pestalozzi was the first man to put into practice Rousseau's theories. But the need for a system of exercise was not fulfilled until the work of German Johann Frederich Guts Muths, much of whose teaching was based on that of the Ancient Greeks and

An acrobat of 1599 jumping through hoops

the Roman Claudius Galen, who had advocated gymnastics for raising the fitness level of the ordinary population. Guts Muths worked for more than half a century in Schepfendal and it was here that he wrote his seminal book *Gymnastik für die Jugend* (Gymnastics for the Young) in 1793. To the exercises of the Greeks he added climbing and balance movements, marching and military drills. He even recommended exercises for the senses, as well as reading aloud and recitation. Following Rousseau's example, he also stressed the importance of handicrafts and gardening. Guts Muths wanted to make young people fond of gymnastics, which he attractively defined as 'labour in the garb of youthful mirth'.

From the theories of Guts Muths gymnastics began its successful development into the sport we know today. His book was translated into French, English, Swedish and Danish, and particularly stimulated – albeit in different ways – two men, who were to have an immense in-

fluence on gymnastics and physical education, which until the middle of this century were almost indistinguishable to the general public. Johann Friedrich Jahn (1778–1852) of Germany and Pehr Henrik Ling (1766–1839) of Sweden had different approaches to gymnastics although they were not as radically diverse as has sometimes been claimed – but their invention and use of the apparatus and methods of training spread the sport throughout the world. Jahn read Guts Muths's book and, in 1811, opened the first outdoor gymnastics centre: the *Hasenheid* on the outskirts of Berlin. Here, on the wooded southern slope of the Spree Valley, he encouraged other young men to exercise twice a week on rudimentary apparatus. The following spring the area was enclosed and the popularity of this *Turnplatz* (open-air gymnasium) grew.

Jahn was partially motivated by patriotism. He smarted under the defeats the divided Germany had suffered during the Napoleonic Wars and was disenchanted with the dissolute life-style he had seen

Above: *Johann Friedrich Jahn (1778–1852) developed many routines for apparatus gymnastics and is regarded by admirers as the father of the sport*

There was a strong moral purpose, for the association's motto was: *Frisch* (alert), *frei* (free), *fröhlich* (gay) and *fromm* (godly); and the initial letter of these four words, in the shape of a cross, subsequently decorated its badges and diplomas.

Jahn was arrested in July 1819 on suspicion of 'secret and most treasonable associations' by officials of the Holy Alliance of Metternich of Austria, and he was jailed for six years. His followers had to be extremely careful and gymnastics, because of its political associations, had to retreat indoors to escape detection. After his release he continued to be politically active, becoming a member of the German parliament in 1848.

His tireless work for gymnastics continued. He founded a large number of

Below: *Pehr Henrik Ling (1766–1839), the Swede whose system of gymnastics was a forerunner of many modern routines*

during his seven-year university career at Halle, Jena and Greifswald. He set out to strengthen the Germans' physique and personality through intensive training. In 1813 Jahn and most of the *Turners* volunteered when German states were again at war with Napoleon. Jahn himself commanded a batallion during the wars and was even a member of the Secret Service. In 1816 he founded the German Gymnastic Association (*Die Deutsche Turnkurst*).

Acrobats of about 1800 balancing on two ropes (from a drawing by Huyot)

clubs and promoted three pieces of apparatus now in standard use in international competition – parallel bars, rings and high bar. Jahn's pupils needed physical strength for lengthy exercises on these apparatus, and the parallel bars were used principally for repetition dips rather than the swinging movements commonplace today.

It was the emphasis on physical strength with which followers of Ling took issue. Theodora Johnson, in *The Swedish System of Physical Education*, voiced a typical criticism when she said Ling's methods 'avoided the fault of the German system, which tends unmistakably to strain the upper part of the body, overwork the heart and lungs, and produce heavy shoulders and stooping gait' – a view of physical education absurd to us now but popular until the Second World War. On the other hand, Jahn's disciples argued that the Swedish system lacked moral fibre.

Ling was originally inspired by a visit to Copenhagen, where he trained at the gymnasium of Franz Nachtegall. After reading Guts Muths's book and founding his gymnasium, Nachtegall was encouraged by the Crown Prince of Denmark (later King Frederick VI), who thought gymnastics might be useful for training his troops. In 1828 the monarch even ordered the inclusion of gymnastics in the school curriculum – a far-sighted enterprise which lost momentum with Frederick's death in 1839.

Ling, however, had already begun adapting Nachtegall's gymnastics for Sweden. He devised such apparatus as the beam, wall-bars, window-ladder and box, founded an institute for the training of gymnastics teachers, established exercise principles for the Swedish Army, and wrote the first section of his book *Gymnastikers almanaa grunder*. Like Jahn, Ling was determined to see his country strong and many exercises were devised for army discipline. Under the original system, a leader took the class in a series of movements which he would select at random. This ensured close attention from the class, strict obedience, promptness of action and mental alertness.

The free flow of movement, whose apotheosis is modern-day women's floor exercises, was the embellishment of some of Ling's followers. Ling's exercises may not have required the muscular force of Jahn's movements on parallel bars, rings and pommel horse, but many of them were even more regimented. Classes usually performed movements by exactly following the leader, and woe betide anyone who was out of step.

The efforts of men like Ling's son, Hjalmar Fredrik Ling (1820–86), another German, Adolf Spiess (1810–58) and Phokion Heinrich Clias (1782–1854) ensured the gymnastic torches of Jahn and Ling were kept burning. It was Clias, born in Boston, USA, but an instructor in Switzerland, who was chiefly responsible for the spread of gymnastics to England. After giving free instruction to boys in an orphan asylum in Berne, he taught gymnastics to the Swiss Army and so impressed English observers that he was invited to London in 1822. A year later he published a book entitled *An Elementary Course of Gymnastic Exercises*.

Among his pupils was Gustavus Hamilton, whose *Elements of Gymnastics and of Callisthenics for Young Ladies* is a classic of the sport. Here, in neat drawings and graphic text, are the exercises popular in Britain at the time. Movements are shown on a leaping stand (a type of spring-board),

high bar, parallel bars, vaulting horse and climbing stand. Women, as the title suggests, are not forgotten. The book describes their callisthenics: 'They are, however, so varied as to suit the gentler manners of the sex, and it is to be found that they confer a grace and ease of action, never before acquired, while they improve the health of pupils, and add surprisingly to the vigour of their constitutions, tending also to reform all deformities, increase growth and confer symmetry of form.'

More clubs opened, including the German Gymnastic Club, using Jahn's methods. The British Army, recognizing the importance of fitness after the Crimean War, formed the Army Gymnastic Staff, later the Army Physical Training Corps, in 1860. One reason for the Army's competitive success in the twentieth century – of which the current national coach Nik Stuart is a prime example – is this long tradition in the sport.

Archibald McLaren, who had studied fencing and gymnastics abroad, was appointed to organize the Army's physical education. His was also the first system to be introduced into British schools, particularly public schools – always in the van of sporting innovation during the nineteenth century. Much of it was military drill and a number of schools employed former NCOs as instructors.

Swedish gymnastics, as taught by Ling, arrived in Britain in 1840 when a Lieutenant Ehrenhoff opened a gymnasium in London. Jahn's methods were unsuitable for girls and the London School Board clearly preferred Ling's system. In 1881 they introduced Swedish gymnastics into London girls' and infants' schools. Centres in Birmingham, Manchester, Liverpool and Bristol also began training teachers.

The spread of gymnastics led to the founding in 1888 of the Amateur Gymnastic and Fencing Association – the two sports were linked at first by their military ties –

and the first national championships were held in 1896, the year of the first modern Olympics, at the Corn Exchange, Northampton. The event was won by Henry L. Cain from the famous Orion Club, Hackney, founded in 1868. Women's national events began in 1924.

But the growth of gymnastics in Britain was less pronounced than overseas. For reasons that are not completely clear, Britain has never been in the forefront of the sport internationally. Gymnastics, even then, could not compete on level terms with home-grown sports like cricket, football, rugby and athletics in the universities and public schools where much of their initial development occurred. It may be that gymnastics was regarded as foreign, or lacking in team-spirit, or simply that it took place indoors and required special equipment. But for whatever reason, Britain lagged behind other countries then and, as we shall see, never really caught up.

In France the link of gymnastics with the Army was apparent with the domination of the famous *Ecole de Joinville*, a military training establishment in south-eastern Paris. The *Ecole* was founded in 1852 by two followers of Francisco Amoros, a Spaniard who acquired French citizenship in 1816 and popularized gymnastics based on apparatus movements and rigid exercises, relieved by singing.

In the United States, as Fred Leonard points out in his valuable book *Pioneers of Modern Physical Training*, the growth of gymnastics in the late nineteenth century was both widespread and intense. The first three gymnasiums were opened in 1825 in Northampton, Cambridge and Boston in Massachusetts, under the direction of three German refugees, Charles Follen, Charles Beck and Francis Lieber. All had left Germany, where they had been colleagues of Jahn, to escape arrest or constant persecution from the policy adopted by the Holy Alliance. Native Americans sub-sequently opened gymnasiums where Jahn's exercises were practised. 'German' gymnastics was the first kind to be established, but other styles of the sport sprang up over the following fifty years. Military Academies, under the inspiration of Charles Alden Partridge, began regularizing drill, and Catherine Beecher started teaching callisthenics for girls in schools in Connecticut. Dio Lewis and Dr Edward Hitchcock, among others, also enjoyed support for their methods.

Ling's gymnastics was promoted by Baron Nils Posse, who went to the United States from Stockholm in 1885, where he was actively supported by men like Hartvig Nissen, Claes Enebuske and Jakob Bolin. In 1889 Dr Edward Hentwell, director of physical training in Boston schools, organized a celebrated conference where the rival claims of Jahn, Ling, military drill and other methods were argued. Predictably and understandably, however, different schools, colleges and gymnasiums continued to use those exercises which suited their particular requirements and wishes.

It was a Swede, de Pauli, who opened the first gymnastics institute in what is now the Soviet Union – in St Petersburg in 1830. But the man who did most to develop the sport was Pyotr Lesgaft, who introduced Prussian drill to the Imperial Army in 1874. Czar Alexandr II eagerly accepted the innovation because of its value for discipline. Lesgaft opposed Jahn's methods, saying, 'exercises which employ equipment involve sharp sensations. They therefore blunt emotions of young people and make them less receptive and impressionable.' The Russian Gymnastic Federation, set up in 1883 on the initiative of a group of social reformers including playwright Anton Chekhov, therefore stressed drill rather than apparatus movements.

The Scandinavian countries, of course, owed much to Nachtegall and Ling, but also to Jahn. Denmark, for instance, used both methods. Countries set up their own federations and associations: France in 1873, Poland in 1867 and Holland in 1868. Germany, where, as we have seen, a federation had already been established, had a reputed 2,000 clubs by 1860. But the most important federation, because of its international repercussions, was formed in Belgium in 1865. In 1881 the president of the federation, Nicolas J. Cuperus, wrote to several European societies inviting them to the federation's festival. On 23 July, the representatives from Holland, France and the two groups making up present-day Belgium – the Flemish and Walloons – met in Liège. This first international convention adopted five main principles: the exchange of documents; rules on mutual invitations; organization of competitions; exclusion of professional gymnasts; and the non-recognition of federations with political or religious goals. It was more a study group for the exchange of ideas than an authoritative body and the major absentee was Germany.

But this meeting of European enthusiasts marked a start, if a hesitant one, of the global administration of gymnastics. It is always taken, rightly, as the beginning of the International Gymnastics Federation (FIG), although the original name of European Gymnastics Federation was only changed in 1921. The earlier date of 1881 makes the FIG, the oldest of all international sports federations, senior even to the International Olympic Committee (IOC).

It is probable that Cuperus, the first president, and his band of pioneers were ahead of their time. Competitive gymnastics, as we shall see, took a long time to become standardized, and there was probably no necessity for any governing body until much later than 1881. As Dr Miroslav Klinger, later a member of the Men's Technical Committee, said, 'We do not believe that even in 1902 the national federations felt like members of an international organization.'

Cuperus himself, a white-bearded, determined man, was indeed always opposed to international competition. 'My idea,' he wrote in 1897, 'is always the same and I look forward to the time when competitions will be unnecessary, the gymnasts receiving the exact amount in health, strength and agility and endurance as the only rewards for their effort. But since, so far, no federation has thought it useful to replace competitions by festivals, I have to yield and take men and things as they are.' One of his gifts, therefore, was this ability to reconcile his idealism with reality. He was to face constant pressure from the French president Charles Cazalet, and also from the revival of the Olympic Games, to accept more whole-heartedly the idea of competition. The international sport was indeed about to begin.

2 International Growth (1896-1952)

The modern Olympics were the inspiration of a French aristocrat, Baron de Coubertin, whose educational theories about the value of harmonizing physical with mental development were similar to the Greek concept. Troubled by the growing commercialism of nineteenth-century sport – and apparently ignoring the fact that many competitors in the ancient Olympics were professional – de Coubertin visualized the setting-up of an amateur championship for the world's sportsmen. At a congress in the amphitheatre of the Sorbonne – in itself ironical because the famous French university has always been so opposed to sport – it was agreed by the seventy-nine delegates and forty-nine sports associations from twelve countries present to re-establish the Games every four years, beginning with a celebration in Athens in 1896. The Pan-Athenian stadium of Herodis, a 2,000-year-old ruin, was restored in white marble.

Gymnastics was one of the nine sports on the programme, although it took over half a century for the sport to be settled in its present format. Women, for instance, didn't compete in individual events until 1952. The FIG didn't run the 1896 contests, which were staged in the centre of the athletics track. Many of the world's best gymnasts did not compete. People just turned up and participated. In these first Games there was no combined exercises competition. But Hermann Weingartner of Germany would have delighted Jahn by proving to be the most adept all-round gymnast. He was first on the high bar, second on the rings and pommels and third on the parallel bars. (The floor exercises were not held as an individual event until 1932.) The rings brought Greece its first victory in the stadium through Joannis Mitropoulos. The official report records: 'Before the result had been communicated to the public, a member of the judging panel, overcome with enthusiasm, cried, "Long Live Greece". Several moments afterwards ... the enthusiasm became indescribable: eyes became wet with tears, hats were thrown in the air, handkerchiefs waved, cheers were prolonged and there was endless applause for which the royal family gave the signal, thus forming an astonishing hubbub.'

There was a combined exercises competition in Paris in 1900, but it included events like the long and high jump, pole vault and heaving a 110-lb weight. Gustave Sandras of France was the winner. One of the difficulties – and glories – of gymnastics in its early days was that it became a test of the all-round sportsman rather than the all-round gymnast. Competitions were added or subtracted almost at will. Gymnasts took part in events in which they had little or no experience, in much the same way as Sri Lanka competitors at the 1978 Commonwealth Games who had never trained on a beam before they arrived at Edmonton. The revival of the Olympics had one striking effect: it stimulated the development and organization of international amateur sport.

In 1898 Cazalet had suggested holding

world gymnastics championships, although they were not then officially given this title which was to be used for the first time in 1934. The suggestion was that the event should be held to celebrate Cuperus's twenty-five years as Belgian president, despite his evident opposition to the tournament. Nevertheless, the first World Championships were held in the Velodrome du Sud in Antwerp from 14–18 August 1903. Four nations – Belgium, France, Luxembourg and Holland – took part. Britain had attended the 1898 congress but did not compete in World Championships until much later. There were twenty-six events at these championships, consisting of compulsory exercises without apparatus, competitions on apparatus, both optional and compulsory, and three athletic events – running, high jumping and weight-lifting.

Two years later Cazalet staged the second World Championships in his home town of Bordeaux, and in 1907 the tournament went to Prague. Still the Germans stayed away, rather like Britain did in the early years of the World Cup in football, preferring a splendid isolation. Germany treated the championships and FIG with resentment. An edition of the magazine *Deutsche Turnzeitung* tried to dissuade non-Slavic countries from participating in the tournament by declaring that competitors might be threatened with violence.

But the championships went on, and were succeeded by those in Luxembourg in 1909 and Turin in 1911. Conditions continued to be haphazard. In 1909 there were compulsory high jumps for gymnasts, who were marked on their style. But the height of the bar was changed without the knowledge of the Technical Commission. Teams often brought their own apparatus which was sometimes rejected by organizers because it did not conform to the norm. It was only in 1949 that the FIG ruled that organizers themselves had to provide the

The Danish men's team performing at the 1908 Olympics at London's White City

equipment. Despite, or perhaps partly because of the difficulties, there were both memorable moments and competitors. In 1911 an Italian dislocated a finger while on the parallel bars. But he held his support position, asked that his finger be reset and, after this was done, dismounted and requested permission to repeat the exercise (then allowed under the rules).

Leading competitors did not necessarily take part in both the Olympics and World Championships as they do today. In this engagingly chaotic era, however, one man stands out – the Italian Alberto Braglia. Born in Modena on 23 March 1883, he was joint champion at the 1906 intercalated Games at pentathlon and heptathlon. He went on to take the combined exercises at both the 1908 and 1912 Games, although he was particularly renowned for climbing a 33-ft rope in one-arm pulls and also for his swinging with straight arms round the high bar (a movement then considered revolutionary). There were no individual Olympic apparatus events from 1908 until 1924. Instead, Braglia won in London a heptathlon consisting of seven individual competitions: high bar swinging movements; high bar slow movements; parallel bars slow and swinging movements; rings stationary; ropes swinging; pommel horse quick movements; and finally rope climbing. Second, only five points behind, was Britain's Walter Tysall, from Birmingham, and English champion for the previous three years.

There was also a voluntary mass-exercises event for teams of between sixteen and forty competitors. The difficulty in judging both the individual and team events

The Danish women's team giving an exhibition at the 1908 Olympics

was already evident. The British Olympic Association official report records: 'The introduction of a recognized code of international rules of judging would be an advantage. Rough and ready methods, even if applied with the most scrupulous honesty, cannot replace the authoritative precedents of accepted work on universally accepted lines.' Recalling the link between sport and military drill, the Association also lamented: 'At present British gymnasts retain the light-hearted spirit of recreation compared to the cold-blooded severity in the case of more military nations.' How often subsequently have we heard similar sentiments expressed?

The 1912 Games were held in Stockholm, home of Ling's gymnasts. The IOC and FIG had gradually come into harmony over control of Olympic competition. These Games were organized under the direction of the IOC but the FIG had real, if unofficial, responsibility for the conduct of events. The Swedish Olympic Committee had originally considered, in accordance with Ling's principles, that international competitions in gymnastics were 'unsuitable', and suggested holding only displays at the Games. The IOC persuaded them to have both. It seemed a sensible compromise. But Germany withdrew from gymnastic events, protesting that the allotted sixty minutes was too short a time in which to complete the competitions and preferring just to take part in demonstrations. So there were a number of exhibitions, including one by Scandinavian women. This incident made a lasting impression on Lord Noel-Baker, the 1500 metres silver-medallist in 1920. He wrote recently in *The Olympic Games* (edited by Lord Killanin and John Rodda): 'I remember the teams of Scandinavian girls, dressed in colourful and lovely costumes, who gave displays of disciplined collective movements, which had the beauty of ballet,

and which seemed somehow imbued with the glorious national spirit of the free and democratic nations of the north.' In the men's team event, Britain finished third – the last medal their men have won in the sport at the time of writing.

Gradually organization became less haphazard. From 1920 the FIG took official control of the Olympic gymnastic tournament and with the IOC agreed that the World Championships would be held every four years from 1922 in the even years between the Games. Cuperus, who had resigned as FIG president in 1924 and died four years later, had lived (probably with mixed feelings) to see gymnastics become an integral part of the Olympics. Cazalet, his successor, paid a tribute to him by saying, 'he relentlessly preached the holy crusade in favour of understanding among gymnasts. It should have been given to him to be present at the brilliant success of this noble cause and, like Moses, to see the promised land on the horizon.'

Competition became more important although Italy continued to be the most successful nation, winning the Olympic team event in 1912, 1920 and 1932. Giorgio Zampori (1920) and Romeo Neri (1932) were the successors to Braglia, now coach to the national team. Their dominance was finally challenged by Switzerland; at the 1928 Olympics Switzerland's Georges Miesz took the overall title and he was to become, with his equally illustrious compatriot, Eugène Mack, the most accomplished gymnast until the Second World War.

Miesz, born in Zurich on 2 October 1904, began exercising in 1922 and was a member of Switzerland's bronze medal-winning team at the 1924 Games. He was to win honours at three more Olympics as he continued his work for the sport as competitor, trainer, propagandist and even as designer of equipment. In Amsterdam he defied the brisk wind which blew across the stadium – Olympic gymnastics always took place outside – to take the overall and high bar titles and silver medal on the pommel horse. Mack may be regarded as the most successful individual male World Championship gymnast of all time. He won five gold, three silver and a bronze medal in a career that ran parallel to that of Miesz, who only took one gold and one silver. Mack's first Olympic title was in the vault at Amsterdam but he is always remembered for his great World Championships in Budapest in 1934, which with thirteen nations attending was the most representative of any until 1954. He took four individual titles including the combined exercises.

Gymnastics was gradually altering. At the 1928 Olympics women were permitted to compete for the first time, having previously been allowed only to give demonstrations. It was admittedly just a team drill event – but it was a start.

The British women's team competing at the 1928 Olympics in which they won the bronze medal

Holland took the title with, in third place, Britain, whose group included such famous female figures of the period as Lucy Desmond and Carrie Pollard. The 1932 Games in Los Angeles marked further progress. Now strictly under the jurisdiction of the International Gymnastics Federation, floor exercises were introduced and, for the first time in Olympic history, individual competitions were held in all apparatus events and also in tumbling, rope climbing and club swinging. The Japanese made their début in the sport and as the official US Olympic report perceptively forecast, 'they made astonishing fine showings considering their lack of experience, and will no doubt rate much higher in final standings at future Games'. Displays were still popular: Mexico performed some dances with demonstrators colourfully costumed as Montezuma's warriors, while the Japanese gave exhibitions of kendo (Japanese swordfighting) and jujitsu, a method of self-defence – judo was introduced to the Olympic programme in 1964. Romeo Neri took not only the all-round title but also

the parallel bars ahead of Hungary's Istvan Pelle, who collected gold medals on the floor and pommel horse. The Americans, who at that stage emphasized individual apparatus excellence rather than overall skill, took the rings through George Gulack.

Women took part in the World Championships for the first time in 1934 in Budapest but had to compete in athletic events for both team and individual titles. Despite the need for solid all-round athleticism there were still signs of how the sport was to develop. Gaki Meszaros, a Hungarian, actually executed a split while posed on the beam! One judge was so surprised (men were still officiating for women's events) that he got up to get a closer look at the feat. She received 9.60. The Czech team were victorious, after having trained for three weeks together to perfect their exercises. Intensive training was arriving.

Nazi Germany staged the 1936 Olympics, their opportunity to show the world their administrative efficiency and physical supremacy. German competitors were rigorously prepared for the event. Alfred Schwarzmann took both the combined exercises and the vault, and Konrad Frey won the parallel bars and pommel horse. Jahn would have been proud of them. Also impressive was Czechoslovakia's Alois Hudec, a masterly winner of the rings with an exhibition regarded as one of the most memorable before the modern era. His inverted crucifix – an upside-down hand balance with arms outstretched – remains the hallmark of a gymnast possessing great strength. He also took world titles on the rings in 1934 and 1938.

For Britain the period between the wars was a depressing one for the sport, with little development or popularity compared

Eugène Mack, the great Swiss gymnast, competing at the 1936 Olympics in Berlin

Many people developed their interest in gymnastics through physical training in the Army. Here prospective recruits exercise at Fulham Football Ground in 1940

to the Continent. This was partly because apparatus gymnastics was of German origin, and partly because of indifference and even rank hostility among physical education authorities. Some recoiled from the muscular stress needed for apparatus work and equipment was even destroyed. The London County Council banned all apparatus from their schools during the 1930s. This followed a disagreement between Madame Osterberg – inspector of PE in schools and a rigid believer in free-standing exercises – and Rudolf Oberholzer. 'Obie' taught apparatus gymnastics in the City of London, but was prevented from expanding his instruction. There was, therefore, little development of the sport in schools, where physical training consisted of free-standing exercises and outdoor games.

As with so many British sports of the era, there was also a lack of contact with the Continent. Not surprisingly no medals were won at the Olympics – except, of course, by the women's team at the 1928 Games. By 1936 Britain had even dropped to eighth place in the women's team event, which now comprised set and voluntary exercises on three apparatus: parallel bars, beam and vault. Women continued to use parallel bars until 1952, when asymmetric bars were substituted and floor exercises added. As for the men, Britain was not even represented at the 1932 or 1936 Games.

The leading British men's gymnast of the period was Arthur Whitford, who collected seventeen national titles over an extraordinary span that lasted until the

1952 Olympics. When he competed in his first English championships in 1928 he weighed 6 st. 13 lb and was so short that he actually had to be lifted up to the high bar. He entered the sport at Sketty Church Lads' Club in Swansea, where he owed much to Walter Standish, a former army PT sergeant and one of the few men to study continental training methods. Standish was the main force behind Swansea's domination of British gymnastics until the mid 50s. After Standish's death in 1939, the tradition was continued by Whitford and Walter Walsh. In the 1924 Olympics four of the eight British gymnasts came from Swansea and twenty-eight years later, five of the nine-strong women's squad and half of the men's at the Helsinki Games were from South Wales.

Interest in gymnastics increased after the Second World War – as it did in many sports – because men had been introduced to physical training in the armed forces. Units like the Army Physical Training Corps in Britain gave more men opportunities and facilities to develop their skills.

The 1948 Olympics, staged in London, further invigorated the sport. Originally the gymnastics was to have been held outdoors at Wembley Stadium, but storms compelled a last-minute switch to the Empress Hall. The entry of sixteen men's and eleven women's teams made simultaneous competition unavoidable. The arena at times resembled a three-ringed circus, with spectators almost cross-eyed trying to watch everything happening at once. The exceptionally high (6 ft) vaulting horse with handles, complemented by a large spring-board, presented an unfamiliar apparatus for many entries. The judging,

Britain's Irene Hirst performs on the beam at the Empress Hall during the women's team event at the 1948 Olympics

Britain's Frank Turner executes a half-level crucifix on the rings during the 1948 Olympics

especially of the women, was still rudimentary. US team manager and former Olympic gold-medallist George Gulack complained: 'A number of officials favoured their own countries and possessed scarcely any working knowledge of the sport.'

Amid all the difficulties Finland, with five gold medals, and Switzerland with three, dominated the tournament – the last time Western countries were to be supreme. Finland, whose men's team averaged 33 years and 7 months, took the team event, with Veikko Huhtanen winning the combined exercises. Josef Stalder was a glorious successor to Mack and Miesz, finishing first on the high bar and performing his famous 'shoot', a clear circle on the apparatus from handstand passing through straddle support. The United States men's team was seventh overall, the highest placing of the non-European nations, although they had two distinct handicaps. The US try-outs were held on 1 May, nearly three months before the Games themselves. Team official Eugène Wettstone complained a number of men were not in top condition when they reported to New York in July to travel to London. Of more lasting and profound importance was the tendency of many Americans to specialize on individual apparatus exercises. Gulack proposed all-round work should be incorporated in national championships.

Another Swiss, Walter Lehmann, 1948 silver-medallist, was to win the combined exercises title at the first World Championships to be held after the Second World War at Basle in 1950. These were the last

The first of the great communist women gymnasts: Helena Rakoczy of Poland, winner of the 1950 World Championships

World Championships to include athletics events. The 1949 congress in Stockholm decided it was too late to alter the programme for Basle, but from 1954 World Championships would only include genuinely gymnastic movements. The congress also decided to introduce a points code for judges to assess the tariff values of optional exercises. The uncertainty before the explosion in the sport's popularity was reflected by the numbers attending the Basle event. Of the twenty countries then members of the FIG only six sent competitors – a total of fifty-eight gymnasts. In the women's event there was a hint of the future when a communist, Poland's Helena Rakoczy took four gold medals, including the all-round title.

3 The Eastern European Takeover (1952-1972)

The 1952 Olympics marked the start of the modernization of gymnastics. The date is not arbitrarily chosen. To begin with, the Helsinki Games saw the first participation of Soviet Union competitors in the Olympics and in no event were their resources more apparent than in gymnastics. They simply transformed the sport. They took five of the top seven places in the men's combined exercises, and seven of the leading nine places in the women's and both team titles. The official 1952 Olympic report records: 'Such physical strength as the Russians displayed on the rings, such hair-fine sense of balance as that which characterized their movements on the pommel horse had never been seen before.' They produced the two overall individual gold-medallists in Viktor Chukarin and Maria Gorokhovskaya, the latter demonstrating her all-round talent by winning silver medals in every event.

Since the 1917 Revolution gymnastics had developed startlingly in the Soviet Union. Marx himself in *Das Kapital* advocated 'bodily education such as is given in schools of gymnastics and by military exercise'. The first national championships were held in 1928 and the following year Radio Moscow started broadcasting morning exercises. The idea quickly caught on. Under the slogan of 'Everything about mankind must be beautiful', factory and college fitness groups mushroomed all over the country. Soon virtually everybody was doing their 'daily dozen' at home or at work. Often there was a ten-minute morning break in factories for compulsory exercises.

The more adventurous exponents progressed to competitive gymnastics. Despite the country's sporting isolation, the standard improved so much that when Russian gymnasts were shown a film of the

Viktor Chukarin, 1952 and 1956 Olympic Champion, began the Soviet Union's domination of the sport

German victories in the 1936 Games, it aroused more amusement than admiration. When Soviet competitors took part in events abroad their talent was indeed evident. In 1937 Maria Tyshko and Nikolai Sery won the gymnastics tournament of the World Workers' Olympiad in Amsterdam.

It was also in 1952 that the Japanese returned to the sport. They were less successful than the Russians – there was a crucial absence of reserves – but their agility was amazing. They might have lacked force in the 'heavy' exercises but they finished second and fourth in the floor sequences and second and joint third on the vault. Takashi Ono, then 31, began his run of superb successes with third place on the vault.

As these new figures arrived, so a number of distinguished gymnasts competed in their last major event. Finland's Keikki Saralainen, who read the Olympic oath in the main stadium on behalf of 5,867 competitors representing sixty-nine countries, had taken part in every Olympics since 1928. Germany's Alfred Schwarzmann, combined exercises champion in the 1936 Games, returned at the age of 40 to take a silver medal on the high bar.

For the first time, there were individual women's floor exercises – an event that was to symbolize the revolution of the sport. Women now took part on the asymmetric bars rather than parallel bars, allowing competitors greater range of aesthetic expression. As the American team manager Roberta Bonniwell pointed out in her official report, 'a new type of interpretative, rhythmic gymnastics has spread throughout Europe in the past four years. It includes to some degree, movements and choreography of dance, and was noticeable in the team drills, free exercises and to some extent on the balance beam. The emphasis is now on beauty, grace and choreography and tends away from strength, power and sustained movements.' The changes didn't please everyone: some critics disliked the way the men's floor exercises were being tainted with 'acrobatics'. But a trend had been set: gymnastics was changing.

The 1954 World Championships in Rome saw the stabilization of the programme as we know it today, with all athletic events withdrawn and the individual events fixed at compulsory and voluntary exercises on six apparatus for men and four for women. The Soviet Union monopolized the men's event, taking the top seven places led by Chukarin and Valentin Mouratov, who tied for first place with 115.45 points. It was also the first appearance in the Soviet squad of Boris Shaklin, ultimately successor to Chukarin but at this stage only fourth overall. The women's events were less one-sided although the Soviet Union still won the team event, led by Galina Roudiko. Only two non-communist competitors finished in the top twenty.

At the Melbourne Olympics in 1956, however, the words of Roberta Bonniwell's report were delightfully illustrated by the arrival of the first internationally acclaimed star of the sport, Larissa Semyonovna Latynina (*née* Dirii). Then only 21, Latynina was to win, before her retirement in 1966, more individual Olympic titles than anyone in any sport. In three Games she collected nine gold medals (a number exceeded by the American athlete Ray Ewry only if the intercalated 1906 celebration is counted). Her total in Olympics, World and European Championships – she missed the 1959 European Championships because of pregnancy and the 1963 competition when the Soviet Union boycotted the event – is a still unequalled twenty-four titles, fifteen silver medals and five bronze. A product of the stark war and immediate post-war years, Larissa was an orphan for whom gymnastics opened a

The Soviet Union's Larissa Latynina, 1956 and 1960 Olympic Champion

door to happiness. Born in the Southern Ukrainian part of Kharsan, the hostilities left her fatherless while her mother, before her early death, worked as a school-cleaner. 'I remember that out of all the dirt, destruction and poverty around us,' she once said, 'there was a terrific urge to make something beautiful. I wanted to be a ballerina and, at 11, I started ballet classes.' The PE programme for girls at school in-cluded callisthenics – the body exercises, in harmony with music, with hoop, ball or sash which are now called rhythmic gymnastics. Her trainer used to make her attend ballet performances and listen to piano concertos. Then she would repeat physically what she had felt. At 16, she became the national gymnastics champion in the schools division. She then gained entrance to a PT college in Kiev where she married Ivan Latynin, a ship's engineer on a Dnieper rivercraft.

Despite a liking for borsch soup and

Two distinguished Soviet gymnasts, Larissa Latynina and Boris Shaklin, are pictured here with their children. Both were Olympic champions in 1960 and also Kiev city councillors

Ukrainian dumplings, Larissa always retained the figure of a ballerina. She was, and in many ways has remained, the classic gymnast, setting a standard by which later gymnasts were measured. As she often admitted, she didn't attempt particularly difficult routines, nor was she especially innovative. Instead, she tried to perfect familiar moves by giving them her own elegant interpretation. Unlike some of her successors, Larissa made gymnastics only part (if perhaps the major part) of her life. She interrupted her career to give birth to Tana and, like Boris Shaklin, she always continued her work as a Kiev city councillor. 'One day,' she recalled, 'I was asked to clear up an argument over places in a day

nursery. I ended up by giving a display. Now the nurses and children alike do their quota of exercises.' Gymnastics made her as popular and famous in the Soviet Union as she was abroad.

Latynina began her triumphant run at the Melbourne Olympics, despite the stern opposition of Hungary's Agnes Keleti. Now 35, Keleti was at the end of a competitive career that would have been even more glorious but for her glaring weakness

Boris Shaklin on the high bar

on the vault. Together with her compatriot, Margaret Korondi, Keleti had consistently presented the most prominent challenge to Soviet domination since 1952. In Helsinki, Hungary was second in the team event. In the floor exercises, where Keleti's fluent moves and easy grace were best exhibited, she was a delightful gold-medallist. At the 1954 World Championships she lost an extraordinary nine marks on the vault, which destroyed her chances of being placed more highly in the combined exercises. But she took the gold medal on the asymmetric bars, silver in the team and bronze on the beam.

Hanging over Keleti's performance at the 1956 Games was the shadow of the recent Soviet attack on Hungary; there would be a parallel twelve years later, with Caslavska's exhibition against the Russians after the crushing of the Czechoslovakian uprising. But this time the gymnastic result was less happy. Another dreadful lapse on the compulsory vault allowed Latynina to overhaul her. Although Keleti's ability in other exercises was equal or superior to the Russian's, Keleti could not make up the difference. Latynina won by 0.30 points. With even a moderate vault, Keleti would have triumphed. Elsewhere she was sublime, collecting gold medals on the beam, asymmetric bars and team drill, and she was joint winner (with Latynina) of the floor exercises. At that most poignant of sporting occasions – the dispersal of the Hungarian Olympic team from Melbourne – Keleti was one of those who remained behind in Australia. Later she went to Israel, where she coached the national team.

Britain sent only one female representative to the Melbourne Games: Pat Hirst, who, despite finishing forty-first, still displayed the 'attack' on the vault which had

Pat Hirst, a record eight-times British national champion

made her a promising track sprinter before the Second World War. Inspired by the 1936 Olympics, she concentrated on gymnastics and competed in three Games whilst collecting eight national titles – a domination unique in British female gymnastics since the war. Her determination in the Melbourne Games, despite all the disadvantages in being the only British competitor, contrasted with the attitude of the German team, who withdrew from the women's events because of the increasing requirement of graceful movement.

The most curious feature of the 1956 Games – in retrospect even more than at the time – was the indifferent display of the Japanese women: in particular, the tiny (5 ft 0$\frac{1}{2}$ in. and 8 st. 2 lb) Keiko Ikeda, who was only thirteenth overall. Gold-medallist on the beam at the 1954 World Championships, she finished third on both floor and beam in 1958, was sixth overall at the 1960 Olympics and 1962 World Championships, led Japan to a bronze medal at the 1964 Games and was still good enough at the 1966 World Championships to be runner-up on the bars and bronze-medallist overall – at the age of 33! It was a career of individual international successes unique in modern gymnastics. If Latynina's peaks were higher, even they weren't sustained quite as long.

But if the Japanese women were off-form at Melbourne, Takashi Ono, among the men, was magnificent, giving Chukarin an epic contest and finally losing the title by only 0.5 points. Chukarin injured his thumb while warming up but kept to his original routine, so displaying the same fortitude he had shown during the war when he fought on the Front against the Germans and was both wounded and

Keiko Ikeda, the leading Japanese woman gymnast for many years, seen balancing on the beam at the 1960 Olympics

captured. Ono was superlative on the high bar where he obtained 19.60 points out of a possible 20.

Chukarin was best on the parallel bars while Shaklin was solid and dexterous on the pommels. Their compatriot Albert Azarian maintained his excellence on the rings – he was to win a second world title two years later and retain his Olympic crown in Rome in 1960 – by using his magnificently defined deltoids to perform his celebrated 'Iron Cross'. His son Edward nostalgically employed the same move at the 1978 World Championships.

The year 1957 was notable for the introduction of the European Women's Championships, to be held every odd year, thus giving gymnastics, with Olympics and World Championships in 'even' years, one major tournament annually. Latynina was now approaching her peak and took all five titles at the inaugural European Championships in Bucharest. The men's event, introduced two years earlier, was held separately, in Paris. Here 23-year-old Joachim Blume, who died with other members of the Spanish team in an air crash in 1959, struck a rare note for Western Europe by beating the Soviet Union's Yuri Titov (defending champion Shaklin was absent) to the overall title and also picking up three apparatus titles.

There was success, too, for Britain. Nik Stuart was second in the floor exercises, the last time any Briton has won a medal in this calibre of competition. He finished only 0.35 points behind Sweden's Olympic Champion William Thorenson and, although he went on to fifth place overall at the 1959 European Championships, his Paris performance was the high point of his career, along with winning the German Turnfest in Essen, 1963, against the best thirty-six gymnasts in Germany. A former parachutist, he became in 1948 an army PTI and used his all-round sports ability –

Japan's Takashi Ono springs off the high bar at the 1960 Olympics. He was twice overall Olympic silver-medallist

he pole-vaulted 12 ft $0\frac{1}{2}$ in. and won the Malayan diving title – to fullest advantage. His slightly impish sense of humour was frequently evident: he was given to crossing parade grounds in a series of front somersaults. His long gymnastics career finished at the age of 37 with the 1963 Britain v. Hungary match at Epsom. Since then he has been a respected and amiable national coach.

If anyone imagined that the Soviet Union had declined with Blume's all-round title at

The Soviet Union's Yuri Titov, 1962 World Champion and former president of the International Gymnastics Federation. 'There is an instant after you have released your grip on the apparatus when you are in the air, free. There is no feeling like it.'

the 1957 European Championships, they were rudely shocked at the 1958 world championships in Moscow. Latynina taking five out of six titles might have been expected; the performance of Shaklin was not. At 26, this unusually large gymnast (5 ft 7½ in. and 11 st.) was now at his peak. He took five out of a possible eight titles –

something which no male has equalled in World Championships to this day. A man of deep concentration and wide-ranging physical ability, he was to retire in 1966 having taken a record ten individual gold medals and three team titles in his twelve-year career.

The Soviet Union had another admirable competitor in Yuri Titov. He took the 1959 European Championships (in Shaklin's absence) and later became president of the International Gymnastics Federation. His feel for the sport has always been acute. 'I love gymnastics', he once explained, 'because I love to fly. There is an instant after you have released your grip on the apparatus when you are in the air, free. There is no feeling like it. If you are trying some new technique there, in mid-air, you will know you have got it right. When you land you don't need applause or a medal – the satisfaction is inside you. You have conquered and it doesn't matter if it is in an empty hall. You have mastered fear, overcome difficulty. You are full of joy.'

With such fine gymnasts as Shaklin, Titov and Azarian available, the Soviets were favourites for the 1960 Olympics. Shaklin indeed took the combined exercises title – ahead of Ono, who was deprived of the gold medal for the second successive Games by just 0.05 points – and Titov was a solid third, but the Japanese filled five of the next six places. Despite their customary slight weakness on pommel horse and rings, Japan took the team title for the first time – and was to hold it for nineteen years. Japanese dominance in this period was based on their high strength-to-weight ratio and a fusion of discipline and spiritual strength. 'The first thing a young gymnast is taught,' explained Sho Fukushini, an international competitor of the period and later Denmark's national coach, 'is how to sit, how to behave himself.' New gymnasts, he continued, sweep the

Albert Azarian using dumb-bells with his son Edward, who was later to become a member of the Soviet team

floors and tidy the rooms of more senior men – to show love and respect for those who have already accomplished more. 'I remember after one exhibition each member of the Japanese team stood up and spoke to the coach. To confess: "You taught me, yet I did it wrong . . . . Forgive me, I am still young, I am not ready for your knowledge . . . . I will work harder and improve." That to me was beautiful. True love between men . . . the love of a master and a pupil. Not homosexual love, but the love of knowledge and respect. I wanted to cry. That to me was real beauty.' Fukushini said that for the whole of his first year in the university squad he spent

Albert Azarian, of the Soviet Union, performs his celebrated 'Iron Cross' at the 1960 Olympics

three hours a day on the parallel bars. 'Not doing skills but just swinging. By my arms. Backwards and forwards. For a whole year, nothing else. This is how I was taught strength, endurance. And obedience.' This policy, inherited from martial arts like judo, kendo and karate, allowed competitors to develop their potential and gave them a monopoly of medals for almost two decades. So the popular, dapper Masao Takemoto, 42 at the time of the Rome Games but still a silver-medallist on the high bar and fifth overall, had a cluster of pupils to whom he could hand over the leadership of the sport.

The 1960 Games were held in the most picturesque setting imaginable: the Caracalla Baths, constructed in AD 217 by Antonius Caracalla, with their arches, vaults and columns. The surprise of the Games was the overall third place of the Italians. They had the foresight to engage Switzerland's Jack Gunthard, formerly a distinguished competitor, as coach and he coaxed the potential from two highly skilled performers who were to be major figures in European gymnastics for two Olympiads: Franco Menichelli and Giovanni Carminucci. Carminucci was to get a silver medal in the parallel bars in Rome and an overall bronze medal at the 1961 European Championships.

Menichelli, then 19, was the superior of the pair. Distinctively dressed in white shorts, rather than conventional tights, and the Italian blue vest, he had what became known as the 'Peter Pan look'. He was as enterprising in action as in appearance. Menichelli was to modernize the floor exercises, becoming bronze medallist in Rome and gold-medallist in Tokyo, and European Champion three times. Before his career ended, when he broke an Achilles tendon on landing from a somersault at the 1968 Olympics, he had shown how tumbling could be fused into an adept and entertaining routine. Previously, tumbling had been too stereotyped to gain the acceptance of most judges, but Menichelli successfully demonstrated its sparkle. Only 5 ft 3 in. and 9 st. 6 lb, he sprang, soared and flipped to the delight of the crowd and introduced the original Arabian high dive forward roll. He was not just an excellent exponent on the floor. He took the combined exercises title at the 1965 European Championships, including further gold medals on rings and high bar.

The United States were making steady improvement. In the Melbourne Games, only one American male had reached the top thirty – John Beckner, who was seventeenth – and no woman was in the leading fifty. By Rome, there were three men in the first thirty and Gail Sontegrath (twenty-eighth) led a cluster of three women to make the first fifty. As Eugène Wettstone pointed out at the time, the United States were still suffering from the disadvantages of being cut off from Europe, where most of the international activity and technical developments were taking place, and also having many collegiate rules which differed from those of the FIG.

Latynina was supreme in the women's exercises, collecting the overall title and medals in all four apparatus finals. But her 24-year-old compatriot Polina Astakhova, graceful and seemingly frail, attracted attention with her charming asymmetric bars routine, where she finished first, and the floor, where she was runner-up to Latynina. The low mark of Ikeda, who had completed a masterly back-straddle over both bars, produced a ten-minute storm of booing but did not influence the judges, who placed her fifth. Eva Bosakova, first of the great Czech gymnasts, won the beam,

The end of Italian Franco Menichelli's career. He broke an Achilles tendon when landing awkwardly during the 1968 Olympics

The Soviet Union's Polina Astakhova dismounting from the asymmetric bars. Only the presence of Larissa Latynina prevented her from being the world's supreme gymnast

showing absolute control while doing the most elaborate turns and agility movements. The beam was to be increasingly used for such agility moves, giving them higher tariff ratings but risking the penalty of one point should the gymnast fall off. Not for nothing do the Germans call it the *Angst Baum* (fear beam).

The trend towards originality continued at the 1961 European Championships, where Latynina took the overall title, 0.30 points clear of Astakhova. Third – and at this stage only one of a number of talented gymnasts – was the girl eventually to dethrone Latynina: Czechoslovakia's Vera Caslavska. She already showed in this tournament the courage which was to make 1968 such a spectacular finale to her career.

Czechoslovakia's Vera Caslavska, 1964 and 1968 Olympic Champion, pictured on the beam

In warming-up for the bars, she slipped and crashed her head on the low bar. The noise was heard everywhere in the Leipzig stadium but, although dazed, she continued competing. In the cluster of superb performances the incident was almost forgotten. It gained greater significance when her whole career was viewed in retrospect.

East Germany produced its first European Champion in Ute Starke, whose determined approach to the board gave her vault – the long arm overflow – exceptionally high flight. Otherwise it was always Latynina and Astakhova who were the most attractively proficient performers. On the beam, Astakhova included a lift from straddled support along the beam to a straight-arm handstand, with her beautiful legs passing through a very wide position. She then slowly levered herself to pass straight-legged *either side of her hands* so her body ended up in a 90-degree position, with her *hands between her legs* – the held lever sit.

On the day of the apparatus finals, an enormous thunderstorm struck Leipzig. Parts of the stadium let in the teeming rain but the championships went on, building up to the climax of the floor exercises final. As Latynina took the stage, the thunder seemed to increase in volume as if saluting the world's greatest gymnast. Suddenly the lighting failed in the stadium, but Latynina continued her routine. As she danced, twisted and tumbled, her moves were sporadically lit up by flashes of lightning from the storm. It might have been a moment from a Wagner opera, so effectively synchronized seemed the stagecraft. The sight of Latynina, graceful and alluring, in this setting a symbol of peace, contrasted distinctly with the turbulence of the weather outside.

The 1961 Men's European Championships were unexpectedly won by Yugoslavia's Miroslav Cerar, whose particular ability on the pommels brought him a further gold medal by 0.95 points. Cerar, 5 ft 8 in. and 11 st. 2 lb, used all his height and strength to best advantage on this apparatus, winning three world titles and two Olympic titles on his. speciality. He floated with stately smoothness round the horse and changed the whole concept of the exercise by occasionally doing high shears – pointing his legs up where previous competitors had pointed them down – as he moved from one end of the horse to the other. He was World Champion, too, on the parallel bars in 1962, although it needed the intervention of the International Federation jury, prompted by the continuous booing of the crowd, to increase Cerar's mark from 9.80 to 9.90 points to defeat Shaklin. At one stage, while the jury was considering the scores, a Yugoslavian official ran to Cerar and attempted to hold up his hand – only to be pushed away. Himself a lawyer, Cerar always respected due process. In the 1962 World Championships combined exercises, Cerar finished fifth in a tournament won by Titov – the man he had beaten for the European title the previous year. Japan's Yukio Endo finished second.

The women's combined exercises went to Latynina, but second (and winner of the vault) was Vera Caslavska, now approaching her peak at 20 years old. She was already a gymnast of four years' international experience, having competed in the 1958 World Championships as the youngest entry. Caslavska, 5 ft 2 in. and 8 st. 9 lb, blonde and immensely vivacious, was to become, by her retirement in 1968, the most popular competitor in the history of the sport.

Once, when she mentioned her hobby was collecting postcards, 3,500 cards arrived for her in three days. Although Korbut, Comaneci and Tourischeva were to over-

Yugoslavia's Miroslav Cerar shows his skill on the pommel horse in which he was pre-eminent during the 1960s

Vera Caslavska displays her four gold medals which she won at the 1968 Olympics

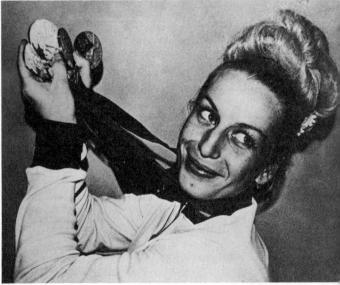

haul her in fame and skill during the following decade, Caslavska continued the trend set by Latynina and carried on by later gymnasts towards making the sport a widely appealing physical expression. She recognized her own place in the development of gymnastics. 'Several times,' she once said, 'I have seen old photographs that show women's gymnastics forty years ago. A lot of people laugh about it now; it all seems very primitive and childish to

Japan's Yukio Endo, the 1964 Olympic Champion, performs on the pommel horse

them but it shouldn't be laughed at. What I do now will surely be surpassed one day.'

Caslavska had originally shown promise as a thin-legged, 10-year-old ice-skater. During the summer she also studied ballet, which taught her a sense of motion and music. She was trained by former world ice-skating champion Dagmar Lerchova. One evening Eva Bosakova, then Czechoslovakia's finest gymnast, appeared on television inviting girls to take part in a national competition to unearth talent. 'Perhaps,' Eva said, 'there is a future World Champion among you.' Caslavska was inspired. She began training under Bosakova, leaving her modest three-roomed flat on the fourth floor of an apartment block in a Prague suburb – her home throughout her career – at 5 o'clock every morning for her first training session. A second session followed school. Success had to be earned.

By the time of the 1964 Olympics, Caslavska was primed to succeed Latynina as overall champion. It might have occurred a year earlier but both the Soviet Union and Czechoslovakia were among the nine countries which had boycotted the 1963 European Championships because the East German competitors were not granted visas by France, the host nation. Caslavska was often adventurous as a gymnast. At the Tokyo Games, for instance, she tried a pirouette off the top bar during the asymmetrics final, and fell – the price of risking more than anyone else. But elsewhere in the Games she showed tremendous zest, leading the Czech team to finish only 0.901 points behind the Soviet Union. The Russian gymnasts were at their best in the floor exercises, where Latynina's mark of 19.599 was the highest of the apparatus finals.

The men's overall title went to Japan's Yukio Endo, who had led the competition by a full point until he fell off the pommel horse in the final exercise. Second, in a triple tie 0.55 points behind, were his compatriot Shuji Tsurumi and two Russians, Shaklin and Viktor Lisitsky. Endo, 27 years old, 5 ft 3 in. and 9 st. 2 lb, epitomized the consummate technique of the Japanese but was endowed with an individual flair the other team members lacked. He made the occasional mistake: apart from his blunder on the pommels he also missed a dismount from the rings, spoiling his chance of a fourth gold medal. Unusually, all the apparatus titles went to different competitors, some justification against criticism that the awarding of separate Olympic medals for all the disciplines was too often an unnecessary reward for closely related physical attributes.

The vault was won by Haruhiro Yamashita, one of the few men whose particular talent now bears his name in the sport. The vault requires unusual arm and shoulder power, together with exact timing, if the necessary height and body shape are to be achieved. When first introduced at the 1962 World Championships, the 'Yamashita' was regarded as extremely difficult to complete successfully, even for men. But now this handspring with a 'pike' (a levering of the trunk and extended legs so they make an angle of 90 degrees or less) in postflight is a standard move – with twists or half twists – for both men and women. The plain Yamashita, indeed, was the women's compulsory vault at the Montreal Games.

By the 1966 World Championships in Dortmund, the Russians, too, had begun to experiment increasingly – particularly on the rings. Here, after the predominantly static work of Chukarin, Azarian and Shaklin, their new star Mikhail Voronin displayed exciting swinging routines. He lived near the Dynamo Football Stadium in Moscow and was originally a gifted

Mikhail Voronin on the rings at the 1966 World Championships when he won the combined exercises

centre-forward. But he was persuaded to take up gymnastics by the Dynamo coach Vitaly Belyayev. In 1966 Voronin was overall champion with 116.15 points, but there was no Russian in the next six finishers. Sergei Diamidov came off the high bar and ended up eleventh, although he displayed a move on the parallel bars to which he gave his name. In the middle of his exercise, with only one hand on the apparatus, he appeared to complete a 360-degree turn in the handstand position. But despite these innovations, the Soviets were beaten by over four points by the Japanese. Shaklin and Titov had now been overtaken by years and younger opponents and neither even reached an apparatus final. Indeed, younger men were starting to improvise moves where their mentors had left off.

It was the same with the women. East Germany's Brigit Radochla had shown in the previous year's Internationals a dazzling variation on the asymmetric bars. She used a daring forward somersault from low bar to high bar with the legs wide in side-straddle position. At the 1965 European Championships, Caslavska had demonstrated her supremacy by equalling Latynina's feat of taking all five titles. In Sofia it was the opening exercise which, as so often in gymnastics, gave a firm indication of the shape and character of the whole event. As Latynina began her floor exercises, her favourite movement, Caslavska prepared for the beam. Latynina, hesitant and occasionally inaccurate, managed only 9.366 points. As the crowd was still pondering the significance of this

Sergei Diamidov, of the Soviet Union, demonstrates the move to which he gave his name during the 1966 World Championships. In the middle of the parallel bars routine he appeared to complete a 360-degree turn in the handstand position

merely adequate mark, a roar of applause broke out for Caslavska's beam routine, worth 9.733. Latynina promptly replied with 9.666 points on her vault but Caslavska scored 9.80. Latynina managed one superb final exhibition on the asymmetrics but Caslavska, showing the hallmark of a great competitor in any sport of always seeming to have something in reserve, was even better. With a breathtaking exhibition, culminating in a backward circle round the top bar and a dismount that propelled her 8 ft from the apparatus, she dismissed Latynina's challenge. This time the Russian had no answer.

But Latynina – and Astakhova too – were obliged to continue in the very winter of their careers. At the 1966 World Championships they reached only one final between them. It was sad to watch Latynina struggle to eleventh place and, in her final international event, see the world team title taken away from the Soviet Union for the first time during her reign. Caslavska was now rampant and it was Czechoslovakia who sneaked the team title by 383.625 to 383.587 points, Caslavska's performances generating in the national team belief in their ability to upset the previously undefeated Russians.

The Soviet Union had prepared a new challenger to Caslavska: Natasha, christened Natalia, Kuchinskaya, a 16-year-old Leningrad schoolgirl, profoundly immersed in the sport. She had begun competing at the age of 12 under the tutelage of her parents, who were both professional instructors, and with the companionship of her sister Marina, a Leningrad girls' callisthenics champion. By the age of 15 she was already a reserve for the Tokyo Olympics and, in 1965, she became European Junior Champion. In the central tradition of Russian gymnastics her floor exercises, although performed to Liszt, unashamedly included the classical poses and swan-like

arm outlines reminiscent of the great ballerina Ulanova. At Dortmund in 1966, Kuchinskaya came close to upsetting Caslavska. Trailing by 0.167 after the first day's compulsory exercises, the pair had an enthralling second-day competition. Kuchinskaya led by 0.034 after the beam. They were level after floor and bars, and Kuchinskaya produced an exemplary vault total of 19.30. Once again the pressure was on Caslavska as she prepared for her final vault – both the combined exercises and team title hanging on her performance. She stood, seemingly for an age, at the end of the run-up. She tapped her feet, looked at the check mark, stared at the horse, and then set off on a carefully controlled accelerating run. She hit the board exactly, hurtled over the horse and landed with a very accentuated forward lean, giving the impression she was about to overbalance. Her supporters' pulse rates suddenly in-

Natasha Kuchinskaya, of the Soviet Union, helps her family with the housework

creased. But they needn't have worried. She swayed backwards. There was no stutter of the feet and as she flung up her arms, a satisfied smile came over her face. Victory was assured.

Kuchinskaya came back superbly in the apparatus finals where she collected gold medals on bars (with 9.80), beam (9.90) and floor (9.90) and a bronze medal on vault (9.666) – each time her mark being superior to the average of her two previous figures for the combined exercises. It seemed as if her ultimate superiority over Caslavska was only a matter of time.

The pair's next meeting was at the 1967 European Championships in Amsterdam. Caslavska faltered on the asymmetric bars, recording 9.40 and, with just the last piece remaining, the scores were Kuchinskaya 29.199 and Caslavska 29.132. Only a steady performance by the Russian on the bars was now necessary for her overall triumph. Kuchinskaya walked to the apparatus with her usual jaunty confidence while Caslavska watched anxiously from where she was about to vault. Kuchinskaya began deftly with a pirouette turn. Then she dropped to the lower bar to begin a long under-swing upstart to catch the high bar – only she didn't. Her fingers never quite wrapped round the apparatus and she slithered to the ground. She stood for a second staring at the top bar and then quickly restarted her exercise. But the zest had gone. She faltered twice more and, when she dismounted, the applause was from sympathy rather than appreciation. The judges' verdict was harsh: 7.766 points and a final place of ninth.

Caslavska went triumphantly on to take the overall title from Zinaida Drouginina, who was unable to sustain her combined exercises performance in the apparatus

Natasha Kuchinskaya performs on the beam. Her career ended early because of illness.

finals: all won by the resplendent, smiling Caslavska. But the Czech girl's most famous victory was still to come. Between the 1967 European Championships and 1968 Olympics, the Czechs under Dubcek practised a more liberal regime than the one favoured by the Soviet Union. In August 1968 – two months before the Games opened – Russian troops helped restore a government more in keeping with Soviet policy. Caslavska, a keen sympathiser with the Dubcek regime, went briefly into hiding, keeping herself fit for the Games by humping bags of coal. When it became clear she was too valuable an international figure to be a target for Soviet oppression, she resumed her ordinary life as a secretary.

The women's gymnastics events in Mexico, therefore, were seen by the world and even by the competitors themselves as an opportunity for Caslavska to show that the hope and spirit of Czechoslovakia still endured. The crowd in Mexico, shoe-horned into the Auditorio Municipal, a steep-banked, splendidly appointed stadium in the centre of Chapultepec Park, did not so much watch the gymnastics as conduct it. Like the chorus in a Greek play they seemed part of the action.

Mexico has always had a flair for the flamboyant and circuses around the world are mostly equipped with Mexican tumblers and acrobats. The city itself is dotted with parallel bars and high bars, and many side streets have tiny parks where children happily learn to exercise.

Ranged against Caslavska were both Drouginina, now married to men's World Champion Mikhail Voronin, and Kuchinskaya, now a year older, more experienced, and winner of both the 1967

The Soviet Union's Mikhail and Zinaida Voronin, husband and wife, and both gold-medallists at the 1968 Olympics

Pre-Olympics title and the 1968 Soviet Championships. A girl of just 16, Ludmila Tourischeva, was preferred (probably because of her age) to the 14-year-old Tamara Lazakovitch, winner of all four apparatus titles at the Soviet Championships that year. Both were to illuminate the sport in years to come. The East Germans even included some 15-year-olds in their team: an indication of how things were to go in the 1970s. *The Gymnast* pointed out that this made a 'mockery' of the British system where gym clubs, run by local PE authorities, were not permitted to enrol children still at school.

The Mexico tournament was as controversial as it was colourful. From the moment Caslavska received only 9.60 points for her optional exercises on the beam – bringing a roar of protest from the crowd – the atmosphere was charged. Berthe Villancher, president of the Women's Technical Committee, hustled over to the judges concerned and, after five minutes' haggling, the mark was changed to 9.80. Kuchinskaya was then probably over-marked on the floor. She lacked the former joyful spring of youth. Her new exercise had a solemn calm coupled with music which failed to add much to the interpretation. She then fell off the asymmetrics, whereas Caslavska scored 9.90 points. The Czech girl, moving with engaging and restrained good taste not always conspicuous in her international successors during the following decade, was immaculate. But despite her clear-cut individual victory over Voronina, even she could not lead her country to a team victory over the Soviet Union, who finished 0.65 points ahead.

In the apparatus finals, Kuchinskaya took the beam, but Caslavska was unbeaten elsewhere to take four individual gold medals and equal the Olympic record of the Soviet Union's Lydia Skoblikova, who took all four women's speed-skating titles at the 1964 Winter Games. The climax of the apparatus finals were, as usual, the floor exercises, in which Caslavska finished equal first with the Soviet Union's Larissa Petrik.

The tiers of the stadium, where Coca-Cola vendors, their wares strapped to their backs, looked like sherpas picking their way up a cliff, were so full that some ticket-holders were forced to sit in gangways to watch Caslavska perform her famous 'Mexican Hat Dance'. Thousands of others were not so lucky and milled around outside or just sat down beneath the trees of the park, happy just to be present at a great sporting occasion. Caslavska's exhibition was everything we could have wished, an effervescent blend of beauty and technical excellence. There were few of the features from ballet in her exhibition that we saw from the Russians. Instead, she displayed a *joie de vivre* that personified her country's hopes. When she finished the noise was that usually accorded to the winning goal in the World Cup Final.

The Mexicans were enraptured by Caslavska and when she married, as the Games ended, Josef Odlozil, Czechoslovakia's 1964 Olympic 1,500 metres silver-medallist, crowds mobbed the pair as they left the Cathedral at Xocalo Square. Caslavska returned to Prague as an international celebrity and presented her four gold medals to the Czech leaders, who had been replaced by the Russian 'puppets'. It was a suitable gesture by a person for whom gymnastics was always more than winning medals.

Compared with this almost-theatrical event, enthusiasm for the men's competition at the Mexico Olympics was understandably more muted. The 22-year-old Sawao Kato succeeded Endo as champion after a tournament that for evenness certainly stood comparison with that of

*Japan's Sawao Kato, the 1968 and 1972
Olympic Champion, on the rings*

the women. After the compulsory exercises, Voronin led from Akinori Nakayama and Kato and, at the end, only 0.25 points separated the three of them. Voronin took the vault final and also the high bar, where he used his patented 'Voronin hop' – a high-piked front vault to re-catch at the other side of the bar. Nakayama showed just how much his country had improved on the 'strong man's' exercises. Japan provided four of the top five places on the rings, including Nakayama, the winner. Now 25, he was steadier than in the 1967 Pre-Olympics, when he muffed his pommel horse voluntary and ended up second to Diamidov. Japan's depth had been amply shown at their 1968 national championships when the top thirty-five men all averaged better than 9.00 on each piece. Here Nakayama had finished first in a competition of intrinsically greater depth than the Mexico Games themselves.

Also in the Japanese team was Mitsuo Tsukahara, the innovator *par excellence*, a man who was to produce a famous somersault from the high bar at the 1972 Olympics and who also introduced, at the 1970 World Championships in Ljubljana, a new horse vault, later to be known as a 'Tsukahara'. This involves a half-turn of the body on to the horse and then, after a powerful thrust from the arms, the competitor completes a one-and-a-half back somersault before landing. With this original move, Tsukahara took the vault in 1970 which helped him to second place overall behind Eizo Kenmotsu, who was having his first major triumph in a long and distinguished career which ended with retirement only in May 1980.

Although Sawao Kato was injured, the Japanese filled six of the top eight places and provided all three overall medallists.

Japan's Akinori Nakayama pictured during his rings exhibition at the Munich Olympics

The Soviet Union, who dominated both the 1969 and 1971 European Championships, had no answer. But if the struggle between Japan and the Soviet Union was familiar, the impact of the Cuban team wasn't. Their floor exercises, in which they threw somersaults 2–3 ft higher than anyone else, showed their talent for the sport. Sadly, they lacked the proficiency to make greater progress during the 1970s. If the Soviet Union was still lingering behind the Japanese in men's gymnastics, it was a radically different matter in the women's, despite the premature retirement of Kuchinskaya, heir apparent to Caslavska. Natasha began suffering from a glandular disease in 1969 and, although she made a brief return in 1970 when she took part in an East German invitation tournament, she finally had to give up the sport.

The Russians had already primed Tourischeva as her replacement but it was now the East Germans, not the Czechoslovakians, who were their principal opposition. As in so many sports, East Germany's clinical preparation and the widespread participation of potential stars brought them to the forefront of gymnastics. At their 1968 national junior girls' championships, there were over 300 competitors with the top ten girls in the Under-14s averaging 9.00, and the top ten in the Under-18s averaging over 9.00 for the four apparatus. From this fertile field of talent came, in particular, three gifted competitors: Karin Janz, Erika Zuchold and Angelika Hellmann.

At the 1969 European Championships, held in the Swedish holiday village of Landskrona, Janz became, at 17, the youngest-ever European Champion. Her flawless technique stood out in an event that saw sixty per cent of the gymnasts with scores of below 8.00 on the beam and only nine competitors reaching 9.00 on the

East Germany's Karin Janz, then only 15, on her way to the asymmetric bars silver medal at the 1967 European Championships

bars. The gamble for high tariff ratings with routines scarcely mastered was not paying off. Janz's fluent swinging and circling on the bars gave her a 9.80 mark and a convincing lead. She finally took four of the five available titles. Although Tourischeva was only equal third (with Zuchold) in this event, she was, in future,

Erika Zuchold, of East Germany, performs on the beam at the 1972 Olympics

to exploit the East Germans' lack of artistic appreciation. However exact the East Germans were, their very efficiency somehow precluded emotion.

At both the 1970 World Championships and 1971 European Championships, Tourischeva was triumphant. Born on 7 October 1952 in Gronzy, Checheno-Ingush, she was to dominate the early 1970s by being unbeaten in every major event until the advent of Comaneci. She was, of course, to suffer for much of this period, despite her superior success, from being a contemporary of Olga Korbut. As my colleague Cliff Temple of *The Sunday Times* once put it: 'However many times Tourischeva may appear to come out of the shadow, it is an illusion, a trick of the light.' But if the fans cheered Korbut, it was invariably the gymnasts themselves who applauded Tourischeva. She was not only closer to the central tradition of Russian gymnastics, with its ballet poses and flowing techniques, but she employed none of the eye-catching ploys of her colleague.

Tourischeva may have been less flamboyant but she was a superior – and more consistent – gymnast. The Russians always cited her in preference to Korbut in propaganda publications like *Soviet Woman* as the ideal Russian female: stable, industrious and reliable. Tourischeva stayed for long periods with her coach Vladislav Rastorotsky, and had a regimented routine that began with a two-hour training session at 6 a.m. In the morning she studied and in the afternoon she trained again. At one stage, she enjoyed reading before going to bed but then Russian scientists discovered it was better to train at this time because the body recuperates more efficiently while it is asleep, thus providing increased benefit

from the training. So she trained in the evening as well. The consistency of training allowed her to overcome her early weakness of falling off the beam, something that occurred at the 1968 Olympics, 1969 Soviet Union championships and 1970 USSR Cup. Tourischeva found gymnastics demanding emotionally as well as physically. 'All one's feeling goes into practising exercises, many of which are set to music. Therefore, somehow dancing with boyfriends doesn't attract me.' She was a propagandist for the sport, maintaining that it was more demanding than ballet. 'At one time I took up ballet but then switched to gymnastics,' she once said. 'You see, our routine is far more strenuous. We do everything ballerinas do and a lot more besides.' Despite this uncompromising exterior, she had a feel for gymnastics which she conveyed to the most experienced of sensitive observers. Pauline Prestidge, the British Women's coach, was particularly moved by her exhibitions, 'which make me want to cry every time I see her perform'. Generous in victory, seemingly unconcerned by the adulation heaped on Korbut, she was also graceful in defeat. One remembers the unobtrusive pat on Comaneci's shoulder at the end of the 1976 Olympic competition more than the publicized kiss on the medal rostrum. Tourischeva particularly excelled on the floor: again the similarity with Latynina, by now the Soviet team coach, is relevant. It was indeed this talent which gave her the edge in her 1970 World Championships combined exercises victory amidst a superb struggle between the Russians and East Germans, who between them collected all the medals except one. The odd medal went, for the first time ever, to the United States, whose competitors had often suffered previously from scoring that did not reflect the often high quality of their performances. Doris Brause received a

Cathy Rigby, of the USA, was the first Western gymnast to shake the communist domination of post-war women's gymnastics

9.766 mark for a sublime asymmetric bars exhibition at the 1966 World Championships. Latynina herself commented: 'What do you have to do to get 9.90?'

The United States' silver medal in 1970 was won, partly thanks to a series of opponents' blunders, by the engagingly pert Cathy Rigby, whose sporting maturity had been glimpsed in her sixteenth place at the 1968 Olympics. At the time she was only 15, then still considered amazingly young for an international competitor. Despite disadvantages in training that included having to start her vault run-up on the pavement outside the tiny Californian Methodist church hall in which she used to exercise, Cathy went on to finish tenth overall at the 1972 Olympics. She then married an American Football player and enthusiastically commentated on gymnastics for ABC television.

The Russians were predictably even more formidable at the 1971 European Championships held in Minsk. Here, in their own country, Tourischeva and Lazakovitch exactly shared all the gold and silver medals between them, having finished joint first in the combined exercises. They were once again the leading two Russians at the Munich Games. But it was Olga Korbut who was to get the publicity.

'I have always been the family baby,' Korbut once said of her upbringing. During the Munich Games she succeeded in generating similar emotions in a widely differing range of people: Soviet soldiers, who wanted pin-up photographs; American matrons, who longed to mother her; and thousands of similarly aged young girls who aspired to Olga's charm. What they apparently wanted to do was to 'protect' her against the vagaries of misfortune and technical imperfection that modern gymnastics can produce. Korbut was indeed popular partly *because* she blundered at crucial moments. When a spectator ran forward to give Korbut a bouquet after her disaster on the asymmetric bars at Munich, she was giving overt expression to every spectator's sympathy. It was something people in more distinguished fields envied. When President Nixon met Korbut at the White House he told her: 'I have always been impressed with your ability to land on your feet.'

The daughter of a civil engineer, Olga had three elder sisters but was the only one with high sporting ambitions. These were originally encouraged by a 1964 Olympic gold-medallist Yelena Voltchetskaya, and later by the unsmiling Renald Knysch, a man whose disagreements with Korbut became notorious. Her principal talent as a gymnast was her originality. Physically she had a particularly flexible spine, which allowed her an enormous range in beam and floor exercises. But, as Larissa Latynina once pointed out, it was not until she began such enterprising movements as her back flip while standing on the high bar to catch the apparatus, and especially her back somersault on to the beam, that she began fulfilling her potential. The back somersault needed incessant practice, but Korbut never allowed this to stifle her zest. Sometimes she would repeat the movement 400 times in a session, yet she retained what Pauline Prestidge termed 'this inner love, this joy in the sport'. Sometimes her inner joy caused her to miss those 400 repetitions and be publicly condemned for her lethargy. Knysch and Latynina exploited her personality. Korbut admitted her choreographer taught her to walk, smile and wink. But she had an instinct as to what would manipulate people's feelings. In Munich, she abandoned her floor composition five days before the competition, and against the advice of her coaches substituted the theme music from the German war-time film *The Woman of my Dreams*. Rampant nostalgia filled the Sportshalle, easily arousing spectators' sentiments.

Korbut was also orginal in that she was successful despite not having the flowing grace, the classical tradition of Russian gymnasts. Rather, she had the movements of a puppet that made full use of her 'chutzpah', the Jewish word for unashamed cheek. The gymnastics world, it must be admitted, has not always shared the public's adulation for its most celebrated publicist. Many esteemed critics considered her skill was not the equal of some of the girls she beat. Instead, she used tricks to sway the judges, already influenced by the response of spectators. Although grateful for the attention Korbut brought to the sport, critics suspected her devotees were more interested in Korbut the person than Korbut the gymnast. Her delight in eating one-and-a-half bottles of tomato ketchup during a meal and her possession of a tape-recorder ('Life is marvellous now because I have a tape-recorder') made her an idol to her fans on the level of many pop stars.

She was virtually unknown when she competed as a 17-year-old in the Munich Olympics, although she had taken her first national title two years earlier. Interest steadily built up over the first two days of the women's team competition. 'Did you see that Russian girl, Olga Korbut, on television last night?' was apparently what people were asking all over the world. After the team event, Tourischeva and Janz were locked for the individual title on 76.85. Korbut had 76.70, only 0.75 points behind after the marks were halved before the all-round finals. A probable medal or a possible gold was there. All three leaders scored 9.65 for the vault. On the bars, after Janz and Tourischeva had recorded the same score as their earlier optional – 9.70 for Janz, 9.65 for Tourischeva – Korbut

Britain's Stan Wild performs the famous vault
to which he gave his name

prepared to compete. But with, it seemed, all the world holding its breath, Korbut demonstrated her attractive frailty.

Her take-off was disastrous. She made mistakes in her early swings and, although she ended magnificently, she received only 7.50. An overall medal was impossible. Although she gained 9.80 on the beam and floor, she finished seventh overall. As Korbut cried, much of the world evidently cried with her. Tourischeva was seemingly unconcerned by all the fuss. She produced a serene floor routine, full of understanding and originality, to finish 0.25 points clear of Janz and take the gold medal.

Korbut was to be more successful in the apparatus finals two days later. But the controversy remained. On the bars Janz, the leader after the preliminaries, gained 9.90 points with her fine methodical exhibition. With everyone, particularly the competitor herself, remembering the blunder in the combined exercises finals, Korbut began on the bars. It was the most splendid of comebacks. The applause was rapturous but the judges only gave her 9.80. For ten minutes the crowd booed, halting the competition as officials bustled to and fro. There was no change in the scores. Still the jeering continued and finally Angelika Hellmann began her routine, only to fluff her landing – and break into tears. The whole incident must have affected the judges. On the beam and floor exercises, Korbut beat Lazakovitch and Tourischeva respectively for the two gold medals with 9.90 – marks that many observers considered were not strictly justified. The world was satisfied but not gymnastics itself.

The men's competition was inevitably less spectacular. Japan, led by the 25-year-old Kato, individual gold-medallist for the second successive Games, won the team title by their biggest-ever margin over the Soviet Union. Despite suffering from a damaged elbow, Kato was under pressure by Kenmotsu, and on his last exercise had to score at least 9.70 to ensure the gold medal. Kato, most distinguished pupil of the foremost Japanese trainer Akitomo Kaneko, responded with a thrilling, swirling routine for 9.75 points.

There was a lack of ostentation about the Japanese: they didn't need to linger in the standing position to receive the crowd's applause after the completion of their exercises, as they were to do later in the 1970s. Nor did they congratulate each other, in attempts to influence the judges' marking. Instead, they would bow, walk with dignity back to their team place, bow to Endo, now the coach, perhaps shake the hands of a team-mate, and then relax before the next routine. They were so much the best team in Munich that it is difficult to determine the reason for their failure to maintain supremacy between 1972 and 1979; whether it was the Russians' striking improvement or even a possible decline of the Japanese themselves.

The Japanese took three of the six individual apparatus titles. Viktor Klimenko, 1973 overall European Champion, was first on the pommels with a stalwart performance, while Nikolai Andrianov, in his second year of competition and at the beginning of an illustrious career, won the floor exercises. He would have been placed even higher in the all-round competition if he hadn't tumbled off the pommel horse. For Britain, Stan Wild, taking part in his second Olympics, may have been ninety-third overall but he received 9.20 points for his innovative vault called the 'Wild', in which he twisted before he reached the horse. Subsequently other more outstanding competitors would adopt the move – a rare moment of impact by Britain on the sport.

4 Worldwide Popularity (1972–1980)

Olga Korbut's performance at Munich had an immense effect on gymnastics. It was the first occasion since the 1960 Games, when televised sport was in its infancy, that the Olympics were shown at peak viewing time in Europe. Britain was typical in its response to Olga's performance. Despite Mark Spitz's seven gold medals for swimming, she was the one who generated most interest in the first week of the Games. The concrete result was evident: young girls queued up to join gymnastics clubs. The British Amateur Gymnastics Association was overwhelmed by the sudden demand for qualified instruction by thousands of girls, their enthusiasm aroused by the vision of Korbut. Many were accepted in club and school gymnastics

Olga Korbut captivated her audience during the 1972 Olympics and here receives a bouquet from a spectator

organizations; many others joined long waiting lists that dampened their ardour. In Britain there were 500,000 participants before the 1972 Games. Five years later, when Korbut retired, there were over three million. In the United States, the number of competitors increased ten-fold between 1970 and 1980. The original problem, US Gymnastics Federation executive director Roger Counsil once explained, was to get the public conscious of the sport and to obtain an identifiable following. Television helped them obtain that. It also brought increasing amounts of private finance as the popularity of the sport grew, climaxing with a Fort Worth industrialist giving the Federation enough land to start building a five million dollar national training centre.

Korbut's first appearance in a major competition after the Olympics (she had, in the meantime, made numerous exhibition tours throughout the world) was at the European Championships at Wembley, in October 1973. She had convincingly won the World Student Games that year: her Yamashita vault had been radically changed and she was now injecting exceptional lift and flight off the horse. She had been involved in an entertaining piece of publicity when the FIG considered banning her back somersault on the beam because of its danger. Korbut, interviewed in *Soviet Sport* on 16 July, said that if they carried out this threat she would retire. The world was aghast at such a prospect: it was like banning Twiggy from wearing a mini-skirt. Finally, the FIG Women's Committee

Olga Korbut, of the Soviet Union, performing her back somersault which was nearly banned because it was considered too dangerous

decided not to vote on the proposal because so many people were against such a stricture.

All was therefore set for the possible revenge of Korbut on Tourischeva at Wembley. Certainly this was what thousands of English schoolgirls, packing the arena, wanted. They were to be disappointed. Tourischeva moved with ease against an opponent weakened by an injured ankle. Sure in all her movements, Tourischeva seemed unconcerned at the attention paid to her more famous but gymnastically less precise compatriot. The pair scored the same marks for vault and bars but Korbut swayed perceptibly on the beam and was less immaculate on the floor. Tourischeva, with 38.10 points, won by 0.45 points. When Olga received her silver medal a rumbling noise, like knee-high thunder, began as hundreds of feet stamped

Soviet coach Polina Astakhova comforts Olga Korbut after her disastrous asymmetric bars routine at the 1972 Olympics

in unison beneath Wembley Pool's banked seats. But Tourischeva was still on the top-most step.

The injury to Korbut had indeed affected her performance. The next day, having aggravated the joint, she swerved off the run-way on her opening vault, dragging her left leg behind her as if she were hauling along an iron ball in a medieval prison. The doctor's inspection was perfunctory: Olga took no further part in the competition. Tourischeva went consummately on to garner all four titles, though she was obliged to share the vault with Angelika Hellmann who, after a mediocre performance in the combined exercises, came back strongly the next day.

Tourischeva admitted afterwards that she was beginning to tire by the time her favourite exercise, the floor, began. She misjudged a descent from a somersault and was momentarily off-balance, being forced to take all her weight on her fingers. She received 9.30. East Germany's Kerstine Gerschau – who, after her overall bronze medal in 1973 at 16 years old, never fulfilled her early promise – produced a captivating routine. Her floor exercises to the Charleston and Black Bottom were full of vivacity and scintillating agility. But she still only earned 9.45 points from the judges, which produced a storm of booing from the crowd. Tourischeva had to rely on the lead from her previous day's mark of 9.60 points to give her the fifth gold medal. It was from similar errors to the one Tourischeva committed on the floor, that the faultless Nadia Comaneci was to benefit when she exploited them in the Russian's final two years in competition.

The Romanian girl, however, was still threading her way through junior events when the 1974 World Championships were held in Varna, Bulgaria. Again, the main interest was the struggle between Tourischeva and Korbut, and again

Ludmila Tourischeva during one of her memorable routines

Ludmila Tourischeva, 1972 Olympic Champion, with her husband Valery Borzov, 1972 Olympic 100 and 200 metres champion, and their daughter Tatyana

Tourischeva was to win. She took the all-round gold medal and gold on the beam and floor, while Korbut was second overall and champion on the vault. Apart from the team title, Russian gymnasts took thirteen of the sixteen medals distributed. Since then things have never been so easy.

'Mass is basis,' explained Yuri Titov, former World Champion and head of the Soviet training programme, regarding their supremacy at the event. 'Russia's success stands on the foundation of physical education for Soviet youth.' The USSR in

Ludmila Tourischeva advises her successor in the Soviet Union team, Natalia Shaposhnikova

1974 had six million gymnasts, 800,000 of them at an advanced stage under constant coaching supervision. There were 1,264 institutes for the training of coaches, with more being opened every month. Over 15,000 girls were 'auditioned' for the compulsory exercises as the build-up to the selection of the World Championship team began.

The outstanding gymnasts were often selected at 11 or 12 years old. The Soviet Union had opened its first sports boarding school in Tashkent in 1962. Soon there were similar schools in each of the fifteen republics. In the gymnastics section at Tallinn, for example, 12-year-olds were spending twenty-five hours on standard subjects and eight hours on gymnastics each week. By 18, they were devoting twenty-three hours a week to sport (nineteen of them to gymnastics) and the same number of hours to academic work.

There is a temptation to believe there is no formal opposition in the Soviet Union to the intensive preparation of children for gymnastics competition, that the greater glory of the state supersedes the individual's welfare. But the official newspaper *Pravda* accused Innokenty Mametiev, the coach

above The Soviet Union's Olga Korbut during one of her unforgettable floor exercises

right Japan's Mitsuo Tsukahara completes a handstand on the rings at the 1975 World Cup

below Czechoslovakia's Vera Caslavska somersaults during the 1968 Olympics

Above The Soviet Union's Ludmila Tourischeva dismounts from the asymmetric bars as the apparatus collapses behind her during the 1975 World Cup at Wembley. One of the hooks had straightened

Left America's Cathy Rigby, beam silver-medallist at the 1970 World Championships and later a television commentator

Below Japan's astonishing Eizo Kenmotsu, an international gymnast for twelve years

Above Romania's Nadia Comaneci, always charming, always precise

ight The Soviet Union was supreme at the 1980 Olympics: lexandr Ditiatin, winner of an unprecedented eight medals one Olympics. No other sportsman has ever won so many

elow right Nelli Kim, 1979 World Champion

elow Elena Davydova, 1980 Olympic Champion, leaps in e air during her beam routine

of Maria Filatova and other exceptionally young gymnasts, of 'crippling children spiritually' by his severe regime and of 'depriving them of their childhood'.

The Soviet Union, with its tradition of ballet, its harsh winters forcing many youngsters to take up indoor sports, and its vast population, has many advantages over other countries. But Titov stressed another important factor in the domination of the Soviet Union: the availability of scientists who do nothing but study the mechanics of the human body in gymnastic manoeuvres. 'It is the scientist who now decides the theory of every development,' he said. 'Then the coaches must teach these new skills . . . and the gymnast must obey.'

If the Soviet Union had vindicated its methods in women's gymnastics, it would have to wait for its pre-eminence among the men until the end of the decade. For the moment, Japan stayed supreme. It was Shigeru Kasamatsu, fifth in the Munich Olympics but now in his prime, who beat the Soviet European silver-medallist Nikolai Andrianov for the overall title. Kasamatsu also secured the floor and vault titles. Only one of the twenty-one individual medals went outside Japan or the Eastern Bloc: the high bar title, to West Germany's Eberhard Gienger. There was a new star on the pommel horse. Hungary's Zoltan Magyar was to prove a most capable successor to Cerar and finish first at subsequent Olympics, World Cups, World Championships and European events until the end of the 1970s.

The pattern for the build-up to the Montreal Olympics seemed set for both the men's and women's events. The men are certainly more predictable because competitors need a gradual build-up of strength and experience to fulfil their potential, and during this development their talent is invariably noted. But with female gymnasts the premium is more on

Japan's Shigeru Kasamatsu, 1974 World Champion

youthful attributes of suppleness and fluency, and therefore new competitors can suddenly spring to the fore. So it was with Nadia Comaneci.

Romania decided to unveil Comaneci to the Western world in April 1975, a month before the European Championships. The event selected was the Champions All, which each spring has been a prominent part of the gymnastics calendar since its inauguration in 1971. Men and women from about a dozen countries compete at Wembley Pool in Britain before capacity audiences. Western nations invariably enter the winners of their national tournaments, whereas communist countries try out promising new gymnasts to see how they respond to the pressures of a high-class event.

At the dress-rehearsal of the Champions All, Comaneci, then 13, was entrancing. The focus of attention before the event had been on the 16-year-old Ludmila Savina, obviously being groomed to succeed Ludmila Tourischeva and Olga Korbut in their Olympic team. But, from the first vault, Nadia demonstrated her ability to equal and often improve on her best training performances in front of large crowds. She scored 9.30 points after two neat Tsukahara vaults. Savina was less exact. On her first vault she ran forward on landing instead of taking the regulation one step. On her second, in an attempt to avoid repeating the error, she leaned too far back and sat down. She received 8.90.

Comaneci was less precise on the asymmetric bars, fluffing her dismount. But, on the beam, she was both inventive and accurate – there was a safely executed front aerial walkover with half-twist – and on the floor she was resplendent. Where Savina was flawless but insipid, Comaneci was flawless and inspired. She showed vivacity and charm, ending the event 0.20 points clear of her opponents.

The Romanian's startling performance was repeated at the European Championships in Skien, a small Norwegian town nestling among the fjords. True, Tourischeva was curiously off-form and Korbut was absent with a damaged ankle, but Comaneci might well have beaten them both, even at their most accomplished.

Tourischeva went astray on the asymmetric bars. Her straddle down with toes surely planted on the bar, hitherto so smooth and clean, was unsteady and one foot was adrift. A few seconds later, a swing to handstand did not quite reach the top and Ludmila, with extreme subtlety, used her 'escape route' and reached her dismount without further mishap. The silence that received her 9.35 mark indicated the crowd's surprised disappointment.

Suddenly, however, the stadium erupted with excitement: Comaneci had scored 9.65 with her floor routine. From then on, she was scarcely challenged. Tourischeva stumbled and swayed on the beam and only recovered her pre-eminence in the floor exercises, where she moved with gaiety and flowing skill to receive 9.80. But the nearest competitor to Comaneci's total of 38.85 was Nelli Kim, the new Russian no.2, with 38.50. Tourischeva was equal fourth.

In the individual apparatus exercises, Comaneci was equally commanding, taking three titles, although the floor exercises were won with zestful precision by Kim. Tourischeva, in her first tumbling stream, flipped out of the square and lost her rhythm. But she still scored 9.55, enough to give her the only medal she was to receive: the bronze. Tourischeva worked hard throughout the summer and, although she lost the USSR Cup to Korbut in July, she had rediscovered her form for the first-ever World Cup in October. This competition was a mini World Championship with the top twelve men and women in the world taking part. But Comaneci wasn't there, supposedly injured after winning August's Pre-Olympics event in Montreal, and Korbut's ankle gave way while warming-up for the floor exercises. This spoilt the significance of the result. Tourischeva was a comfortable winner with four out of the five gold medals, including the overall title, despite near-catastrophe on the asymmetric bars. As the Olympic Champion dismounted, one of the hooks on a tensioner straightened, causing all the apparatus to collapse.

However, even such an admirer of the Russian as Pauline Prestidge was convinced in 1975 that Comaneci was the premier competitor. 'But Nadia is so precise technically. She is doing movements on the beam that ten years ago would have been attempted only on the floor. And her bar routine and vault are the best we have seen. She has even more fluency on her back somersaults than Olga Korbut but does not pause either before or after her movements.' Comaneci was born on 12 November 1962 and, as a 4-year-old, was already jumping on the furniture like a frustrated trampolinist, a tiny bundle of restlessness. In 1968 Romania launched a sweep to find the most promising gymnasts and train them in sports schools. One of those who began searching for potential competitors was Bela Karolyi, a former football player, whose wife Marta was a noted gymnast. 'She was a gymnast and since I fell in love with her I fell in love with her sport.'

Bela said he used to wander round Gheorghe Gheorghiu-Dej, a town of 40,000 in the foothills of the Carpathian Mountains. One day during school play-time, he noticed two girls running and jumping, pretending to be gymnasts. When the bell rang they disappeared and, although Bela searched for the pair, he couldn't find them. He returned twice to the school without finding them. On the third occasion he went into one class-room and asked, 'Who likes gymnastics?' The two girls sprang up, crying, 'We do.' One became a promising ballerina. The other was Nadia, then 7 years old.

What impressed Karolyi was her courage. 'She loved to fight. She would fight anyone.' This, together with her natural aptitude, allowed her to compete within a year at the National Junior Children's Championships. She was thirteenth and Karolyi bought her an eskimo doll to ward off bad luck. 'I told her she must never finish thirteenth again.'

Was Nadia exceptional at the beginning? Karolyi was once asked. 'No better than many. The important thing is, she is exceptional now.' By 1971 she had made her junior international début in the Friendship Cup in Bulgaria, winning both the bars and beam. Two years later, she was competing against seniors. Karolyi always coached Comaneci although he never tried to smother her opinions. Often when journalists approached him with questions about her form, he would prefer Comaneci to answer. Comaneci, herself, made the change from nonentity to celebrity with quiet distinction. She developed both physically and mentally. Between 1976 and 1980 her physique filled out, her sharply-etched ribs climbing in steps up to her deep chest and wide shoulders. But she never lost a lissom charm that often enraptured observers. She strove for originality. Her dismount from the asymmetric bars during which she completed a high twist and then a back somersault was one example of this.

If the Soviet Union no longer possessed the world's finest female gymnast as 1976 began, they at least had Nikolai Andrianov, who was destined to take the Montreal Olympic title and, at 23, was strong enough

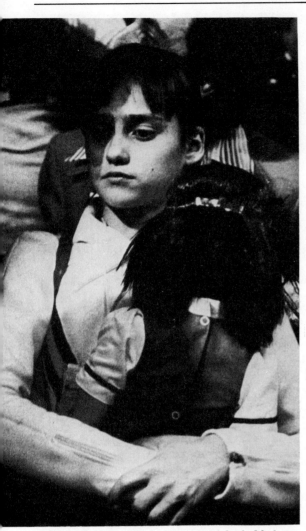

Nadia Comaneci looks uneasy as she holds her doll at the 1976 Olympics – but she has just won the combined exercises gold medal

affection from many spectators. I her career this was going to chan now it was left to Miss Kim, winne USSR Cup the previous May, to spectators how well technical ex can be blended with charming gra received 10 out of 10 for the floor ex in which she was a superb succe Latynina and Tourischeva. Coman first on both the bars and the beam Olga Korbut, in her final comp

The Queen hands over her crown. Ludm Tourischeva kisses Romania's Nadia Co the Russian's successor as Olympic comb exercises champion

the four routines, whereas Olga Korbut lost as many marks on just the vault. The Russians may have retained their team title, but the cheering for Comaneci as she collected her silver medal made the gold-medallists look aside with embarrassment and mutter among themselves.

Despite her precision, there was a lack of warmth about Comaneci in Montreal, and her clinical perfection did not win

to cope with the rings agility of youth. At th Championships in Bern solidly through to win t three apparatus gold masterly performance b silver-medallist Eberha promise of the tall 17 Alexandr Ditiatin.

Born in Vladimir o Andrianov had improv his international débu medal that year in the I ships, second in 1973 1974 World Champ winner of the 1975 I ships and World C close to his peak for He did not try o routines, preferring awkward movement even if they didn't He was nicknamed ' coaches because of h to keep his legs strai difficult movemen innate sense of co-o was still remarkabl been precociously first coach record sport: 'Nikolai joined. Medium a fidgety and stubb only finished tw Junior Champions verance eventuall precedented run

In Montreal he Soviet Union tea the Japanese, de of reigning W Kasamatsu, who operation. After

Nikolai Andriano World Champion,

Avril Lennox, Britain's premier competitor of the 1970s

received a silver medal: a deserved rather than nostalgic tribute from the judges.

Avril Lennox, probably Britain's most effectively consistent woman gymnast of the 1970s, reached the overall final finishing thirty-fifth. Her steady determination brought her four consecutive national titles, and an OBE, although she was rather too heavy physically for international competition.

The slimness of Comaneci, the absence of any physical signs of puberty despite her being 15 years old, aroused rumours that have never been stilled. Some people in the sport, including France's Dr Robert Klein, chief medical examiner at the 1978 World Championships, and the president of the Danish Gymnastics Federation, Niels Peter Nielsen, have stated drugs may

have been used to slow the physical development of Eastern Bloc competitors. Klein suggested the possible use of 'brake drugs which act on the pituitary gland' to allow female gymnasts a higher strength-to-weight ratio than if they attained puberty.

On a more pleasantly human topic, both Korbut and Tourischeva retired to marry after the Games: Korbut (who had apparently turned down five boyfriends) to Leonid Bortkevich, lead singer with the Russian pop group Pesnyany, and Tourischeva to Valery Borzov, the 1972 double Olympic sprint champion.

Their retirement left a gap in the team which only a country with as much talent as the Soviet Union could fill. By the time of the 1977 European Championships in Prague, Elena Mukhina and Maria Filatova were challenging Kim's position as the premier Soviet gymnast. Mukhina had a superb bars routine, including a Korbut

flip from the top bar (but performed with a full twist) and a back somersault dismount. In the combined exercises, Comaneci was clearly dominant despite some controversial judging. She totalled 39.30 to finish 0.35 points clear of Mukhina. The following day disputes over marking continued. After Comaneci had been placed second on the vault and asymmetric bars, the head of the Romanian delegation was called to the phone to speak with Bucharest. On his return, the Romanians abruptly left the competition to express their disgust. A special jet was flown from Bucharest so the team could leave Czechoslovakia immediately.

However, there were numerous, more objective observers who considered Comaneci's 9.85 for an earlier floor routine generous. But the incident unmistakably highlighted a lack of consistency in the judging. Sometimes the judges were clearly influenced by the crowd or the reputation

Olga Korbut and Leonid Bortkevich, lead singer with the Russian pop group Pesnyany, exchange wedding rings at their January 1978 wedding

of the competitor, and they seemed to give preference to some teams. This problem has not altogether been solved. Controversial judging occurred again at the 1978 World Championships, held at Strasbourg, that charming town of waterways and quiet alleys. There was a new Comaneci, 4 in. taller and 21 lb heavier than at Montreal. She was now a woman rather than a girl. She had become a more alluring figure, but we learnt that week how perfection in women's gymnastics can be blemished by maturity. Comaneci lacked her old power-to-weight ratio. She remained a great gymnast but the extra weight and inches had handicapped her more than it would a gymnast who relied less on precise skill.

Natalia Shaposhnikova demonstrates her celebrated one-hand swivel on the beam

The Soviet Union's Elena Mukhina, the 1978 World Champion. Her career, and nearly her life, ended in 1980 when she injured herself in a vain bid to compete in the Moscow Games

In addition, Nadia seemed to have lost some of her desire for victory and, at times, she seemed uninterested in the event, seeking to spend long periods with her new boyfriend, 21-year-old Kurt Szillier, the Romanian champion. Ironically, the draw selected the Soviet Union to compete first on the asymmetric bars and Romania on

the beam, so the order was exactly the same as in Montreal. The similarity was almost uncanny. Nadia's routine seemed as fluent as ever – but wasn't there a sway there, a foot out of line here? Unlike the Nadia of Montreal, she didn't wave to the crowd. She ran off the platform. The Russians, who had been sitting down to watch Comaneci after completing their bar exercises, got up confidently. They knew already that the Romanian was vulnerable. The scores only confirmed it. In Montreal she began with 9.90; in Strasbourg it was 9.75.

Half-way through the compulsory exercises, the Romanians protested against the low marking of Comaneci, implying that they would repeat their walk-out of the 1977 European Championships if they weren't satisfied. This support certainly aided Comaneci on the floor, where her unexceptional routine with notably low jumps brought her 9.70. It didn't aid her on the asymmetric bars, where she actually fell off. She was fourth overall but still retained enough to take the beam title.

The new champion was Elena Mukhina, now 17 and a girl of tremendous concentration. Brought up in Moscow by her grandmother after the early death of her mother, she began gymnastics at the comparatively late age of 9, but six years later was Soviet Junior Champion. Her total of 78.735 in Strasbourg was 0.20 ahead of Kim, who said with sincere pleasure, 'I feel my second youth has just begun.'

But Mukhina's special skill on the asymmetric bars – including a full twist in a standing somersault from the top bar to re-catch – could not deprive the United States of its first women's title in Olympic and World Championships history. This went to Marcia Fredericks, a 15-year-old from Connecticut, who scored a perfect

Marcia Fredericks, of the USA, startled everyone by winning the asymmetric bars at the 1978 World Championships

Kathy Johnson, of the USA, bronze-medallist on the floor at the 1978 World Championships

10.00 points on this apparatus at the 1978 World Championships. Her superbly original optional routine – rewarded with 9.95 points – was completed with clean dexterity, while her colleague, Kathy Johnson took a floor bronze medal.

The United States were equally impressive in the men's competitions. Kurt Thomas captured his country's first Olympic or world title since the 1932 Games with a masterly display in the floor exercises. He exploited his ideal physique – 5 ft 5 in. with short legs and long arms – to perform an enterprising routine that included a flashy series of swinging leg moves known as the 'Thomas flare', performed with equal facility on the pommel horse and floor. Three two-hour sessions a day at Indiana State University and the constant support of his wife Beth provided the background to his victory. By the end of the championships, even the Japanese official Masahide Ota admitted his competitors 'should be as original as Thomas'.

It was much needed advice, because the Japanese barely beat the Russians – the points were 579.85 to 578.95. The men's competition was dominated by Andrianov who, with one stunning exception, was impeccable. The exception was on the pommel horse, their opening event in the team competition. Andrianov actually came off the apparatus, an incident even more extraordinary in retrospect than it seemed at the time. He received 9.05 and retired red-faced to compose himself.

Everyone momentarily thought they were watching a slow-motion repeat of the incident because Vladimir Markelov, the European Champion, then did exactly the same. It must have been a severe blow to the morale of the Russians after their high expectations of defeating the Japanese, who

Three great gymnasts pictured together at the 1978 World Championships. Left to right: Japan's Eizo Kenmotsu, second overall; the Soviet Union's Nikolai Andrianov, first; and Alexandr Ditiatin, of the Soviet Union, third

had no adequate replacements to compensate for the retirement of Sawao Kato and Mitsuo Tsukahara ('After 30 I can do the warm-up or the competition but not both'), the runners-up to Andrianov in Montreal.

Instead, the Russians had to be content with Andrianov's overall supremacy in taking the individual combined exercises. Despite the physical disadvantage of stiff shoulders, he finished ahead of the ageless Eizo Kenmotsu, with Ditiatin in third place. The apparatus titles were evenly spread among the leading competitors, with no single entry winning more than one title.

Britain, too, had a modest but pleasing success when Ian Neale became only the second-ever Englishman to secure an FIG

pin. That international performance was complete justification for his decision to give up work and rely on his savings, sponsorship, the salary of his wife Barbara, and the encouragement of coach John Atkinson. 'This performance,' he said, 'put the full stop to the sentence.'

If anyone thought the 1978 World Championships had seen the end of Comaneci's career, they were mistaken. By the 1979 Champions All, Comaneci had once again altered her bodyshape.

Romanian team officials dismissed her weight increase between Montreal and Strasbourg as 'puppy fat' and said Nadia had a 'new determination' for the sport. 10 lb lighter than at Strasbourg and looking well-tuned for the event, she was a clear winner of the title, finishing 0.35 points clear of the Soviet Union's Elena Naimoushina. The Soviet coaches watched the rejuvenated Comaneci, competing in her first international event of the year, with evident concern. Only a sway on the beam, where she landed unsteadily from a tuck-back somersault, blemished a performance that was both effervescent and original.

A month later came the European Championships in Copenhagen, from which only Nelli Kim of the top Russians was absent. But Mukhina was there, and also Natalia Shaposhnikova, an 18-year-old, now rapidly fulfilling her potential with a unique balancing act on the beam, on which she performed a one-handed handstand, twisting her body until it was horizontal. There was also a melodious floor routine to Tchaikovsky's 'Nutcracker Suite'. Advised by Vladislav Rastorotsky, who coached Tourischeva, Shaposhnikova was described in training by the former Olympic Champion as 'prickly as a hedgehog. One never knows what to expect from her.'

But neither Mukhina nor Shaposhnikova could match Comaneci this time. Indeed, it was another Romanian, Emilia Eberle, who was second overall, with Shaposhnikova third, a distant 0.70 points behind Comaneci's winning score of 39.45. Not only did the Romanian carry off the all-round European title but she won the vault and floor exercises, curiously enough the 'weakest' of her movements at the Montreal Games, and was third on the beam. Despite Shaposhnikova's victory in July's Spartakiade and Kim's return to finish

second equal with Eberle in the World Cup behind another Russian, Stella Zakharova, Comaneci was favourite for the World Championships, taking place for the first time in the United States. The decision at the 1978 FIG congress to hold World Championships every odd year meant that the event would be staged in 1979 to establish the sequence. It was a dramatic, often controversial competition in the big, brash Texas town of Fort Worth that saw Romania snatch the women's title from the Soviet Union – only their second defeat since 1952. But Romania's triumph was achieved with limited help from Comaneci. An infection in her left hand forced her to enter hospital after the first day of compulsory exercises. The next day her hand was swollen to nearly twice its normal size. She continued competing – and even received 9.95 points for the beam – before returning to hospital to have an operation on her hand to drain the infection.

Of more lasting controversial significance was the whip-cord appearance of the Romanian team, particularly Comaneci. Rigorous dieting may have been only the least dangerous of the methods employed to fine down the competitors to such a degree. It may have made them more efficient gymnasts but it also left them frighteningly emaciated. Melita Ruhn (third), Rodica Dunca (fifth), and Eberle (seventh) were all inspired; whereas the Soviet women, with the exception of Kim, were sometimes slipshod. With Mukhina slightly injured and therefore unselected, and Shaposhnikova nursing a damaged ankle, the Soviet Union suddenly found gaps in their talent. Three competitors slithered off the bars – and the Romanians were home first by just 0.625 points.

Kim, however, was unbeatable individually. Now 22 years old, she took the overall title with 78.65 points. Her self-possessed maturity was never so evident as at the press conference after her victory, when she pleaded for a change in the lower age-limit for major international events from 14 to 16. 'It is not good,' she said, 'that a child, during puberty, should undergo such nervous tension and continual, intense physical training. In competitions, this tension is sometimes so strong the feminine grace disappears, to the benefit of pure acrobatics.' Kim's statement was so forceful because she made it after having become World Champion – a triumph of a distinguished and highly popular girl after six years of competition.

The Soviet Union's Maria Filatova receives some final attention to the ribbon in her hair from her coach, Galina Mamentyeva, before an International Moscow News tournament

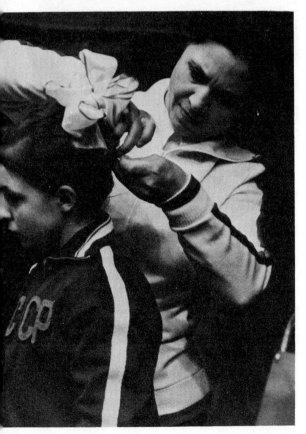

Born of a Korean father and Russian mother in Shurab in the eastern region of Leninabad, she always retained her attractive Oriental looks. She was athletic in childhood, often playing football with her brothers. Like so many leading communist competitors she was selected for a sports school after some basic tests to assess her potential for gymnastics. This occurred when she was 9 years old in her new home town of Chimkent, and she was a member of the Soviet team by 16 when she competed at the 1974 World Championships in Varna. There, she introduced a 540-degree whirl during the floor exercises, a hazardous move which caused her to damage her foot and fail to make the last thirty-six in the combined exercises. But her insistence on originality, particularly on the vault, led her to challenge Comaneci for the Montreal all-round title. Pleasantly shaped for a height of 5 ft 2 in., her elegance on the floor and infallible technique made her a worthy successor to Tourischeva. She benefitted from the use, for the first time, of orchestrated music for the floor exercises: something that extended the range of all the competitors in their interpretation of movements, and provided varied enjoyment for spectators.

Despite receiving some notoriously low scores from Eastern European countries, China made a very encouraging return to the sport after seventeen years' absence from the International Federation. Their joyful daring brought the competitors tremendous applause and one gold medal: Ma Yan Hong's asymmetric bars title, shared with East Germany's Maxi Gnauck. Britain continued a steady improvement by finishing sixteenth with Susan Cheesebrough, Suzanne Dando, Denise Jones and Mandy Goval receiving FIG pins for their totals of over 72.00 points. The surprise of the women's events was the indifferent performance of the Americans,

Above: *Kurt Thomas prepares to catch the high bar*

Left: *Bart Conner, together with Kurt Thomas, led the US revival in the sport*

only sixth overall and with no individual medals. Deprived of the injured Rhonda Schwandt and under-age Tracee Talavera, and with Kathy Johnson still recovering from injury, three US competitors suffered the ignominy of falling off the beam in front of their home crowd. It was even more startling given the performance of their male team, which replaced Japan as the greatest threat to the Russians. Although Japan did indeed finish second

Above: *Bart Conner during the routine which won him the parallel bars title at the 1979 World Championships*

Right: *Kurt Thomas, of the USA, second overall at the 1979 World Championships*

overall in the team events, they only took one other medal: Koji Gushiken's bronze in the pommels. With Andrianov now being overhauled by younger athletes, the Soviet domination was led by Alexandr Ditiatin, with Alexandr Tkachev taking third place with some superbly original moves on the high bar and parallel bars.

But they had to be at their best to match Kurt Thomas and Bart Conner, who between them picked up three gold medals, three silver and a bronze in individual events. As Thomas said of the US progress: 'For so long, our flag has been down in the box somewhere during the medal ceremonies. Now it was up there almost every time. It was a great feeling.' The British maintained their standing by finishing eighteenth overall with Tommy Wilson the highest placing at eighty-second equal.

5 The 1980 Olympics – and after

The year 1980 was remarkable for the Olympics and the Games themselves were remarkable because of the absence of many countries, who responded to American President Jimmy Carter's call for a boycott. The Games had been awarded to Moscow in 1974. Although several organizations, particularly Jewish ones, then and subsequently protested against the staging of the Olympics in a country where individual freedom was repressed, the opposition was rare and comparatively muted. Most politicians and, in particular sports administrators – unfortunately not always sensitive to their responsibilities as human beings – ignored their complaints. There was always the distinct possibility that between 1974 and the 1980 Games the Soviet Union would attack another country. Twice in the previous twenty-five years, they had done so during Olympic year itself: Hungary in 1956 and Czechoslovakia in 1968. In December 1979 the Soviet Union sent troops into Afghanistan to shore up a crumbling communist regime.

Three weeks later, Carter, his prestige low in the United States, called for a boycott of the Games. It was a sound political move because it wooed American voters in the year of the presidential election, cost the United States little money, and struck a blow against the Games which the Soviet Union had always been using for propaganda purposes. For four months until 25 May, when acceptances for the Games had to reach Moscow, debates raged. On the one hand, politicians were content to end the ambitions of thousands of young people, who simply wanted to compete against athletes from other countries. On the other, sports administrators and particularly the competitors themselves, refused to admit that political and moral responsibilities should *ever* supersede sporting ambitions – one could imagine with what enthusiasm some might want to play sport with Nazi concentration camp guards.

As the Soviet Union refused to withdraw their troops from Afghanistan, saying that they had been called there (as had the United States in Vietnam fourteen years earlier), Carter tried to get the Games moved from Moscow and also stage rival 'free world games'. Both ideas failed. But he was able to persuade the United States Olympic Committee to decline an invitation to Moscow. The USOC curiously offered little resistance, possibly because they knew that without Federal support they couldn't stage the 1984 Games in Los Angeles. The decision ended for ever any treasured notion in America that the USOC was an independent body. Other nations joined Carter's boycott, particularly those which relied heavily on American aid, such as West Germany and Japan.

But Carter failed to elicit the hundred per cent boycott by Western countries which he had hoped for and probably expected. Most Western European Olympic committees went to Moscow, although many of their nations' governments applauded Carter's stand. For this the British Olympic Association must take much blame or credit, since it was the first Western European country to stand out quite firmly against the boycott.

In all, eighty-one nations, five fewer than at the Montreal Games which had been affected by the Black African boycott, went to Moscow, with some sports suffering more than others. Gymnastics was savagely hit in the men's events but scarcely blemished for the women. Among the men's teams, those from Japan, second at the 1979 World Championships, the United States (third), China (fifth) and West Germany (seventh) were missing from Moscow. Ordinarily, the absence of Japan would have been crippling. But from the team which lost the world title to the Soviet Union both Shigeru Kasamatsu and Eizo Kenmotsu had retired. The new team was still being prepared. Although Koji Yamawaki and Koji Sotumura, two graduates from Nippon University, had been impressive at the Olympic selections in March, it was absurd to believe they would have adequately filled the gap in the old team.

The real loss was the United States, for both Kurt Thomas and Bart Conner had shown in March's American Cup in New York that their performances at Fort Worth were being splendidly sustained. Thomas received a perfect 10.00 on the high bar and won the combined exercises, with Conner in second place. Behind were such distinguished performers as Bulgaria's Stojan Deltchev and Hungary's Zoltan Magyar. Thomas dominated the competition with five titles, to bring his total of gold medals in American Cup competitions to twenty-seven. Conner campaigned vigorously against the boycott and this prevented him from devoting sufficient time to training. When he went to London for April's Champions All he was below form, finishing second to East Germany's Lutz Hoffmann. He was even slipshod on the parallel bars on which he

Bulgaria's Stojan Deltchev produces a fine high bar routine at the Moscow Games

was reigning World Champion, failing to fix two movements and scoring only 8.80 points.

One American not glimpsed at Fort Worth, because at 13 she was under-age, was being assiduously prepared for the Olympics: Tracee Talavera. The minimum age for women's senior international gymnastics was then 14. In 1980 it was increased by the FIG congress to 15 to take effect from the 1981 World Championships. Talavera's victory in the American

Cup over Romania's Emilia Eberle confirmed her steady improvement since she first became interested in gymnastics after watching Olga Korbut at the 1972 Olympics. She began exercising when she was 7; 'The first three years were sort of fun and it didn't matter how I did. It is still fun, but now I have to do well in meets and things like that,' she said in the spring of 1980. She had left her home town of Walnut Creek, California, in 1978 to stay with Julie and Dick Mulvihill at their gymnastics academy at Eugene, Oregon, a move that understandably aroused in her conflicting and unresolved emotions: 'I thought it was neat, being away from Mum and Dad and things. But after a while you sort of realize . . . .'

Her routine there was rigorous: exercising in the morning, schoolwork in the afternoon and then more training in

Romania's Emilia Eberle helped Comaneci in their country's sustained challenge to the Soviet Union

the evening. But it helped her to finish third in the 1979 American Cup and improved her floor exercises, which in the early days had always been a weakness in her programme. Her mother, Nancy, took a secretarial job to help pay for her upkeep and instruction. The problem of financial support that Western European gymnasts face when compared to their communist counterparts was outlined by Mulvihill as he prepared Talavera for the 1980 Games. 'We have to bust our tails to survive; they don't have to worry about apparatus or about salaries. That's what gripes me when Carter says he'll move the Olympics to some other place and give 300 million dollars towards doing it. Well, hell's bells, why doesn't he give the athletes 300 million dollars? Then we would beat their asses.'

Talavera, probably the most outstanding female talent the United States has ever produced, and the Chinese, who had been so impressive despite lack of experience at Fort Worth, were the significant losses from the female tournament, which centred on the form of Nadia Comaneci. For five weeks after Fort Worth she was unable to train as she recovered from her hand infection. But then she began the slow build-up towards Moscow, introducing a number of new moves for the Games, including starting her asymmetric bars routine with a mid-air somersault to catch the lower bar.

The odds were always against her in Moscow, as Bela Karolyi admitted, with the home crowd likely to influence the judges to favour the Russian gymnasts. With her great rival, Nelli Kim, retiring after the Games, it seemed as if Comaneci, now 18, would also make this event her last major international, particularly since two months after the Games she was starting a four-year course training to teach sport. The strain, too, of keeping her weight down must have begun to tell, although she looked slightly heavier than in Fort Worth. Karolyi, however, insisted that not only was she the same weight as in December 1979, but she planned to continue competing after the Olympics.

The Soviet Union had an immensely talented team, despite being deprived of Elena Mukhina through a grave injury. Three weeks before the Games, Mukhina had been practising alone – against strict instructions from her coach – and had fallen on to the back of her neck from the asymmetric bars. She was taken to hospital with a paralysed upper spine. The severity of the accident was shown by the fact that specialists from Minsk, Leningrad and Moscow all attended her. During the weeks of the Games, rumours were rife

that she was dead, but Soviet authorities denied them and several Russian newspapers printed interviews with her. Yet the gymnastics began under a shadow.

Mukhina might well have been omitted from the Soviet team; her accident happened at a time when she was making a desperate last attempt to earn selection after finishing well down the field in May's USSR Cup. This event had been splendidly won by Elena Davydova, who climaxed her performance with a perfect 10.00 on the floor. In 1976 Nelli Kim had shown she was the Soviet gymnast in form by winning the USSR Cup two months before the Games and then being the highest-placed

Nelli Kim, the Soviet Union's 1979 World Champion

Russian in the Olympics. In 1980 Davydova was to do the same thing. Born in Voronezh on 7 August 1961, she had been a member of the Soviet team since the age of 14, when she became the Soviet asymmetric bars champion. She was second in the Soviet Union Championships the following year but she didn't sustain this early promise. She wasn't even picked for the World Championships in either 1978 or 1979 and only re-emerged from a cluster of seemingly equally talented competitors in the spring of 1980.

Davydova had been carefully shielded from overexposure before the Games and had plenty of time to define her distinctive style. She had always been an individualist,

Elena Davydova, the Soviet Union's winner of the 1980 Olympic combined exercises title, springs on to the horse during a vault

Elena Davydova during her delightful floor exercises routine

beginning alone at 6 years old in her home town of Voronezh when she saw on television two Soviet Olympic gold-medallists of the 1960s – Natasha Kuchinskaya and Larissa Petrik. She immediately started practising the exercises, seeing if she too could do the 'splits'. 'You mean,' I once asked her, 'you began alone at home?' 'Da, da' (Yes, yes), she answered enthusiastically, her round face beneath the pageboy haircut suddenly coming alive.

By the time she was 7 years old she had entered the Soviet system for producing potential internationals and had begun exercising at school. A year later, she was attending a specialized school and was being trained by Ena Korshunov and then by her husband, Gennadi, whom Davydova describes as 'my second father'.

Her willingness to take risks gave her a margin of supremacy in Moscow. Such risks included a double somersault during the floor exercises, performed so deftly and fluently that she continued the movement without pause. Davydova relished danger. Her favourite relaxation was motorbike racing and she enjoyed driving her father's car. 'It helped calm my nerves,' she said, 'after all the big international tournaments.'

Nelli Kim, her marriage unsettled, was no longer the outstanding competitor in the team. But she was utterly reliable and would not err as other Soviet gymnasts had done at Fort Worth. The only other major absentee from the Games was Czechoslovakia's Vera Cerna, who had injured herself in late June and was unable to go to Moscow. After finishing sixth overall at Fort Worth, she would surely have been prominent again.

For the second successive Olympics, an ice-hockey stadium was used to stage the gymnastics, the proximity of the seats to the covered rink providing the setting for an intense atmosphere. But this was rarely generated. Not only was the 12,000-seater stadium sometimes only two-thirds full but the crowd, although surprisingly well-behaved considering the controversies they observed during the tournament, seldom became involved in the action. The boycott insidiously lessened the impact of the Moscow Games even when they weren't directly affected. The women's tournament was a case in point. There were few really memorable moments; nothing to stir one as deeply as Vera Caslavska's 'Mexican Hat Dance' in 1968, Olga Korbut at Munich, or the first perfect 10.00 in the Olympics by Comaneci in Montreal.

The lukewarm interest was apparent on the opening day of the women's competition when there were only about 8,000 people present: this for an event that would normally pack most stadiums and in a country where gymnastics has such a supposedly strong and winning tradition. Unfortunately, the Romanians and Russians were drawn in separate sessions of the first day. Although this allowed one to scrutinize each team individually, it meant there was no genuine confrontation. Comaneci began on the compulsory exercises as if her form were as immaculate as ever. But she seemed curiously withdrawn. She skipped off the stage after her routines. When she received 10.00 on the beam – her first perfect score since the 1977 European Championships – surely she was entitled to return to the podium for a smile and a wave? But she preferred to remain amongst the Romanian team, who, goodness knows, needed her enough after their flawed exhibition.

If Karolyi was encouraged by Nadia Comaneci's first-day performance, after which she was joint leader alongside Shaposhnikova with 38.85 points, he must still have been dispirited by the team's showing. Dumitrata Turner fluffed the bars, receiving 9.15 points, while Melita

Nadia Comaneci looks under pressure at the 1980 Olympics

East Germany's Maxi Gnauck, joint second overall at the Moscow Games and 1981 European Champion

Ruhn, third at Fort Worth, was only seventeenth in Moscow after the first day because of a number of imprecise routines. After the opening day, the Soviet Union with 197.75 points had a 0.95 point lead over East Germany, and Romania was 0.10 points further back. The Romanians' chance to upset the Soviet Union once again had gone.

Comaneci's opportunity to win the combined exercises vanished when the voluntary movements began. She was in the lead overall as she started her smooth, easy routine on the bars. But, as she reached up to transfer her grip on the top bar, the apparatus slithered through her hands and she fell backwards on to the floor. There was hardly a sound in the arena as even the Russians looked up with surprise. Nadia shook her legs, quickly recovered her composure and went on to complete the exercise. But, as we suspected at the time, her Olympic title was destined to slip away from her. She received 9.50 points for the bars, instead of her expected 9.90 or 9.95, and at the end of the first day she had dropped to fourth place, with Maxi Gnauck taking over the lead. In fact, Davydova was only fifth at this stage but Comaneci's blunder allowed her no further margin of error or leniency from the judges.

The Soviet Union competitors, revelling in the lack of opposition from Romania, were expansive on the floor. None of their six competitors merited less than 9.90 points and Davydova's striking routine of verve and versatility gave her a maximum 10.00. The one sad note was that they all used a medley of tunes to accompany the range of their interpretations of physical movements. There was no longer the easy flow and harmony of the floor exercises of the 1960s and early 1970s when only one piece of music was used.

The Soviet Union was never troubled in the team event, with five of their competitors in the top eight and the sixth, Elena Naimoushina, in twelfth place. With a total of 394.90 points they won the title by 1.40 points from Romania. The East German team was third.

Natalia Shaposhnikova on the asymmetric bars

Nadia Comaneci balances on the beam during her controversial routine which provoked a major row at the 1980 Games

Three Soviet competitors – Shaposhnikova, Davydova and Kim – went through to the combined exercises final to face the double-pronged challenge of Maxi Gnauck and the Romanians, Emilia Eberle and Nadia Comaneci. It was amazingly close, with Davydova owing her victory to her consistency. She never scored less than 9.85 points. Maxi Gnauck made a hash of the vault, meriting 9.70 points; Natalia Shaposhnikova received only 9.75 for the floor; Eberle fell off the beam; and Comaneci became the centre of a controversy notorious even in a sport which, because of the difficulties of marking, is always rife with rows. At the end, only 0.125 points separated the top four competitors and it was this closeness which made even the slightest difference in marking immensely important. Comaneci made two imperfect vaults for a best mark of 9.75 points. But she was masterly on the floor (9.95) and bars (10.00). This meant that on her last apparatus, the beam, she needed 9.95 points for the gold medal; 9.85 would give her joint second place with Maxi Gnauck behind Davydova. Her routine lacked its usual composed precision. She swayed unmistakably on the beam and her dismount was slightly askew.

There was a long delay over the marking, ending finally with a judges' conference called by Romania's Maria Simionescu, the head judge, who was supervising the marking with the aid of a video camera. Only competing countries can have officials at the Olympics and, because of the boycott and because there is, in any case, a shortage of properly qualified officials, the judges on this apparatus were all Eastern European. According to Ellen Berger, head of the FIG Women's Technical Committee, the Bulgarian gave Comaneci 10.00, the Czech 9.90, and the Soviet and Polish officials 9.80. With the top and bottom scores being discarded, the two other marks

Officials argue over the worth of Comaneci's mark. In the centre Ellen Berger, head of the FIG Women's Technical Committee, makes a point to Romania's Maria Simionescu, the head judge on the beam

would then have averaged out at 9.85. But Mrs Simionescu refused to register the mark, claiming the score should be 9.95. The crowd remained remarkably passive, which was astonishing considering how the combined exercises title depended on the verdict.

Mrs Simionescu could not persuade the judges to alter their scores and eventually Mrs Berger entered the dispute. She supported the judges, telling me the next day that, in her opinion, Comaneci's performance was worth 9.85 points. With the backing of Yuri Titov, re-elected the week before as FIG president ahead of American Frank Bare, she insisted Mrs Simionescu register the mark. All the while, Karolyi talked to officials in an attempt to influence their decision. Eventually Mrs Berger ordered the competition controller to register the mark and the score of 9.85 was flashed on to the scoreboard. The crowd cheered and Karolyi made signs of disgusted disbelief. The Soviet Union had

the gold medal for which they had craved and Comaneci had been dethroned.

The controversy over the marking aroused fears that the Romanians would repeat their famous walk-out at the 1977 European Championships in Prague. But, presumably because this would have been too great an insult to the fatherland of communism from a satellite country, or because this would have endangered their future participation in events, the Romanians stayed in Moscow. Yet the reactions to the evening's performance were spiteful, showing how deeply the antagonism was rooted. Karolyi declared it was 'all a plot' between the Russians and Poles, whereas Mrs Berger said Karolyi had unfairly tried to influence the officials. Nor was the controversy over. It was to become more mysterious the next night, when the apparatus finals were decided.

For Eastern Bloc countries the Moscow Games were a mighty display of propaganda and of solidarity amongst friendly nations. It was important that nothing should be allowed to spoil this communist carnival and that all the favoured guests should go home relatively content. With the Soviet Union, the host and mother country, assured of the premier title – the combined exercises – the lesser prizes were now to be doled out. The necessity of restoring calm to a fraught situation may explain what occurred the next night. On the beam, where the same judges were officiating as on the previous evening, there was a dispute over the marking of the Soviet Union's Natalia Shaposhnikova. This time, it appeared, Mrs Simionescu succeeded in restricting the mark to 9.85 points, which gave Comaneci her first gold medal of the tournament.

But far more extraordinary was the scoring in the floor exercises. Here, Comaneci initially received 9.90 points and Nelli Kim, giving a glimpse of her most

Nelli Kim during her floor exercises routine

delightful form, took 9.95 points – and, we believed, the title. But just before the medal ceremony, Comaneci's mark was changed to 9.95 to give her a share of the gold medal with Kim. Mrs Berger said this was because a British judge, Susan Thomas, had inadvertently registered 9.95 instead of the intended 10.00, to make Comaneci's average 9.95 and give her a total of 19.875 – level with Kim. But other officials said the Romanians had lodged an official protest at the original mark and the Jury of Appeal raised the mark for the only time in the Games. Furthermore there was no incorrect button-pushing by any British judge.

On the final night the marking seemed far stricter than previously, with only two competitors, Kim and Comaneci, scoring 9.95 points. No one else received higher than 9.90, although Maxi Gnauck produced a delightfully deft bars exhibition which scored 9.90 points – a performance not noticeably less valuable than her routine two days earlier, awarded 10.00.

The vault gold medal went to Shaposhnikova. Although she scored only 9.825 on the final night, it was 0.50 better than anyone else. Both Gnauck and Comaneci sat down on landing. It was scarcely surprising that, after so unsavoury a week's gymnastics, Franklyn Edmonds, president of the BAGA, was eager for the FIG to scrutinize the incidents to prevent any repetition. Edmonds suggests that no coaches should be allowed to talk to officials and the chief judge should be, if possible, from a neutral country.

For Britain, Susan Cheesebrough, who had been the most successfully consistent gymnast since Avril Lennox's retirement, began safely on the compulsory exercises, achieving a fine 9.50 points on the beam, but she fell away badly on the optional exercises, reaching only 9.00 for the floor. Instead, it was Denise Jones, with a preliminary total of 36.425 points, who was the highest-placed of the British competitors after the first two sets. Her best performance was a neat beam routine, in which she scored 9.20 points, although she nearly missed her footing as she prepared to dismount. All three British girls qualified for the final and Denise Jones was best-placed in twenty-third position. Suzanne Dando determinedly recovered from a lapse on the asymmetric bars to total 70.775 in twenty-seventh place, while Susan Cheesebrough was twenty-eighth with 70.725.

The men's competition was completely dominated by the Soviet Union – in particular, by Alexandr Ditiatin, who won eight medals, more than anyone else has ever achieved in one Olympics. American swimmer Mark Spitz, with seven golds at Munich, and Andrianov, with seven medals at Montreal, had previously been the most successful competitors. Ditiatin used his unusual height for a gymnast of 5 ft 9¾ in. to obtain a range of movement and amplitude which offset the disadvantages of his long levers. He totalled 118.650 points to take the combined exercises title, including a 10.00 on the vault, the first perfect mark in men's Olympic gymnastics history.

Even Kurt Thomas would have been unable to match Ditiatin in this mood, for the blond Russian gave massive evidence that he was the finest male gymnast of all time as he demonstrated his skilled versatility to obtain medals on all six apparatus, again a unique achievement in the sport. Born on 7 August 1957, he began gymnastics almost as a remedial exercise because at the age of 8 he was stoop-shouldered and his father took him to a

Nelli Kim on the beam at the 1980 Moscow Games

local gymnasium to try to improve his physique. He had always been noted for his stubborn determination and he overcame a weakness on the floor through constant practice. He used his height as an ally in his performance to give him a clear-cut definition of movement in many exercises. But his rise was only gradual. Fourth in the Montreal Olympics, third in the 1978 World Championships, he took the World Cup in 1978 and 1979 before winning the world title at Fort Worth. Fond of reading and a student at the Leningrad Institute of Physical Culture, he is an ideal sportsman for the Soviet Union, an example of hard-earned success through intelligent work.

It was expected that Alexandr Tkachev would press Ditiatin closely but he made a number of grave errors, even on his favourite apparatus, the high bar. During the compulsory exercises he caught his foot on the bar, ruining his routine. Yet on the team voluntary exercises for this apparatus, he scored 9.95 points and then, in the combined exercises final, a maximum 10.00. Because of his original blunder, however, he didn't qualify for the high bar final – a pity, since he is probably the most proficient performer in the world. Mikhail Voronin, who directed Tkachev's training after the death of his original coach, Pyotr Korchagin, insists technical flaws rather than any psychological weakness make his performances erratic. With Tkachev also making a bad mistake in his compulsory floor routine, it was Andrianov who pressed Ditiatin most closely.

Making a sustained comeback after

Left: *Alexandr Ditiatin, the Soviet Union's winner of a record eight medals in one Games, during his high bar routine in Moscow*

Right: *Alexandr Tkachev, of the Soviet Union, performs on the high bar*

finishing eighth at Fort Worth, Andrianov was always close to his compatriot without ever leading the competition. In what was probably his last event before retirement, he was never flurried, never hurried, always precise, and succeeded in taking two golds, two silvers and a bronze. This brought his total to a record thirteen Olympic medals, three more than Boris Shaklin aggregated. Both Soviet gymnasts have taken part in three Olympics.

Hungary's Zoltan Magyar ended his superb career by adding to it yet another pommel horse title. His consistent strength and dexterity brought him marks of 9.90, 9.95, 10.00 and 10.00 in his four exhibitions. Using the 'Thomas flares' (which he terms the 'bouncing wanderer') in his voluntary routine, he whirled round and along the apparatus for one of the most memorable performances not only of The Games but of the decade.

The British men – Tommy Wilson, Keith Langley and Barry Winch – began poorly on the rings, presumably through nerves. But they improved throughout the competition to put up one of the best performances by a British men's team for many years. For once there were largely competent performances on the pommels. Although Langley scored only 8.65 points on this awkward apparatus in the optional exercises and 8.40 on the parallel bars, he received 9.70 for the vault. In the combined exercises final, Winch was the highest-placed at thirtieth, and Wilson came thirty-first, only 0.50 points behind. Langley, still erratic with an excellent but generous 9.90 points on the vault and 8.45 on the bars, was thirty-fifth.

The most disturbing feature of the Games was the increasingly dangerous

Hungary's Zoltan Magyar, supreme on the pommel horse, unbeaten between 1973 and 1980, retired after the Moscow Games

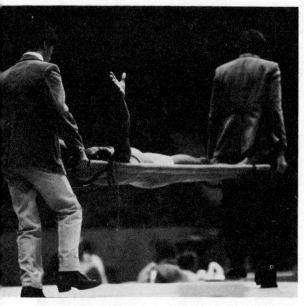

Cuba's Jorge Roche is carried off on a stretcher after damaging his back during the vault

The Soviet Union's Nikolai Andrianov waves goodbye as he retires after finishing second overall at the Moscow Olympics

routines of many gymnasts. Mukhina's accident has already been mentioned, but the superb Cuban, Jorge Roche, tried two-and-a-half back somersaults on the vault and didn't quite complete the last turn. He landed on the back of his neck and was carried off to hospital. As the need for originality has become more and more pronounced, gymnasts are increasingly adventurous, often risking their safety. Competitors and their coaches will always seek ways to improve performances, whatever the consequence, and often the danger becomes normal for the competitor. 'After a while,' Nadia Comaneci says, 'if you work on a certain move consistently then it doesn't seem so risky. The idea is that the move stays dangerous and it looks dangerous to my opponents – but it isn't to me. That is my secret.'

The Soviet Union competitors wave to the crowd after winning the 1980 team gold medal. Nadia Comaneci looks on

Although she did not compete in either the World or European Championships in 1981, Miss Comaneci was always present in spectators' minds, always the centre of speculation. There was no official announcement of her retirement, a decision made all the more likely by the defection to the United States of Bela and Marta Karolyi in April 1981, together with the Romanians' top choreographer Geza Pozsar. Although they had ceased to be Nadia's personal coaches they still controlled the Romanian team and remained inevitably a close and persistent influence over the girl they had introduced to the sport. The Karolyis abruptly left the team during a tour of the United States and, after initial difficulties in securing suitable teaching posts, settled near Houston where they finally became both part-owners of a club and instructors at San Houston University.

Although dethroned at the Moscow Olympics, Miss Comaneci remained the world's most celebrated gymnast, a natural attraction for which tournament organizers were often prepared to pay 'appearance' money. The Romanians were rumoured to have asked for £20,000 for Nadia to compete in the European Championships in Madrid. Both Romanian officials and Titov said the news had been invented and that her absence was due instead to her participation in Labour Day Celebrations in Bucharest. With Nelli Kim now appearing only in exhibitions and Elena Davydova unselected, East Germany's Maxi Gnauck was scarcely challenged.

Still only 16 but with two years experience of major international gymnastics behind her, Miss Gnauck used her extreme suppleness and unusually long legs for someone of only 4 ft 11 in. to compile a dazzling asymmetric bars routine which earned her the highest marks of the four apparatus – 19.95. Although particularly proficient on the bars, for which she got a perfect ten, she also took gold medals for the beam and floor exercises as well as the overall title. She lacked however the natural grace and elegance of gesture to make her readily appealing. Two of the Soviet Union's competitors both untried in major events, continued the trend towards smaller and smaller competitors – Alla Misnik (4 ft 6 in. and 4 stone 12 lb) and Olga Bitcherova (4 ft 5½ in. and 4 stone 8 lb).

Miss Misnik was third overall but Miss Bitcherova was more noted for her size than her placing because she was only twenty-third overall after a mistake on the asymmetric bars. Six months later she would be the most unexpected of world champions.

The men's event, held in Rome, finally and justifiably saw the overall victory of Alexandr Tkachev. With Bulgaria's defending champion Stojan Deltchev injured and Alexandr Ditiatin unselected because he had been studying for exams, Tkachev seemed to revel in the responsibility as his country's premier competitor and as favourite for the overall title. Although pressed by both his compatriots, Yuri Korolev, second, and Bogdan Makuz, third, he made none of the mistakes which had affected him in the past. Now 23 and an international since 1976, he had benefitted from the conscientious coaching of Mikhail Voronin, who had discovered him

Yuri Korolev, 1981 World Champion

in the early 1970s in the village of Semilouki, close to Voronej. Particularly skilled on the high bar (a speciality of Voronin himself), his leap over the apparatus to recatch was invariably completed with deft efficiency.

The World Championship men's events, held in Moscow in November, seemed likely to be dominated by Tkachev. But instead it was Korolev, only preferred at the last moment to Artur Agopian at the European Championships, who made the most progress over the summer. He had dominated the 1980 European Junior Championships in Lyon and his rise was maintained in 1981. Two months after the European Championships he was first equal at the World University Games. In Moscow he excelled in the Olympiski Hall where 23,000 people, a record world championships attendance, watched the final day's competition to provide an atmosphere both more fervent and nationalistic than that experienced during the Games a year earlier. Like Andrianov he was born in the old Russian city of Vladimir and was, like his predecessor, a difficult pupil – Soviet coaches frequently relate for public consumption how people become champions only through overcoming character deficiencies. Obsessed with football and with little inclination for studying or training assiduously, Korolev only reached the promised land which awaits all good communist competitors when he eliminated any vagaries of personality.

But he was aided by an ankle injury to Ditiatin who struggled to thirty-sixth and last place in the Combined Exercises Final. Makuz, Korolev's predecessor as European Junior champion, had taken the lead after the parallel bars and high bar and then, on the last exercise, the pommel horse, scored a solid 9.90. It seemed enough for victory because Korolev was less adept at the pommels than on other apparatus. However Korolev, moving with unusual amplitude, spun round the horse with the control of Zoltan Magyar himself and received, deservedly, 9.95, his highest-ever mark for the event. Two days later Ditiatin obtained some revenge by capturing two of the apparatus gold medals with Korolev taking only one. The Soviet Union's victory in the team event had been totally assured by their placing four men in the top four places, a domination which even the Japanese, second in Moscow, had never enjoyed. China demonstrated their continuing improvement by finishing third, only a lack of exactness in the completion of their exercises preventing them from a higher placing.

The Chinese were even more impressive in the women's competition, finishing second overall and, even more pleasingly and surprisingly, securing their silver medal with a team that was both remarkably tall and mature. Wu Jiani was 15 years old but the others gave evidence of a refined grace that was especially striking in its unfamiliar originality because it came from a country who had competed in only one World Championships in most people's memory. None other than Ludmila Tourischeva, now an esteemed official, applauded their success 'for they prove one can still succeed without having a very low centre of gravity. I personally support the type of gymnastics which does not exceed a certain amount of acrobatics and risks because then one can still say: what a lovely sport gymnastics is.'

There was a freshness in their approach that might have received even higher recompense than the team silver medal, two apparatus silver medals and one bronze, but for the uniformly exceptional display of the Soviet team. With Nadia Comaneci only watching the event and Maxi Gnauck injuring an ankle during the team floor exercises – although she recovered in time for the apparatus finals to win splendidly the beam, asymmetric bars and vault – there was no stopping the Soviet Union who completed the first team double since 1958. They even filled the top six places, a monopoly unprecedented in women's gymnastics history.

Although Davydova led the qualifiers into the Combined Exercises Final she stumbled from a twisting back somersault off the beam and received 9.50. This allowed 15-year-old Miss Bitcherova, who a month earlier would have been too young to compete, to build on her perfect vault mark of 10 and compile 78.400, with Maria Filatova again having to be content with the silver medal. With Miss Davydova getting the bronze, the Soviet Union ended with 20 of the 45 medals. Even such a responsible writer as Michel Thierry in *L'Equipe* asked whether there was not a danger in such a universally practised sport for one country to dominate all aspects of both the men's and women's sport.

More pertinent and even more pressing was the problem of the size and age of the competitors. Yuri Titov blamed the coaches 'who wish to go too fast' in the development of their gymnasts but this scarcely provided a practical solution. The disadvantage of the trend towards tiny competitors dominating the women's sport is that we have been losing the presence and appreciation with which a fully developed woman can infuse her exhibition. Instead competitors are now too often performing like puppets. The International Federation should perhaps consider whether two weight divisions should be introduced, not solely to make titles accessible to everyone but to retain a brand of gymnastics to which the sport owes its popularity. Raising the minimum age limit of competitors to 16 might help

Olga Bitcherova on the beam on her way to becoming 1981 World Champion

but then Miss Filatova for instance only grew four inches between the 1976 Olympics and the 1981 World Championships when she was 20 and still only 4 ft $10\frac{1}{4}$ in. tall. She remains unusually small – her mother incidentally is scarcely any bigger – and this, as we have seen, is of immense help in the sport.

Perhaps the best solution is to modify the method of marking, reducing the value of risk (worth 0.50 points) and substituting a bonus for aesthetic appreciation. This would help older and larger competitors to compete on more even terms with gymnasts like Miss Bitcherova, restore, at least partially, the kind of gymnastics we enjoyed in the 1960s and early 1970s, and most important of all, reduce the risk of accidents. Even Titov agrees that the 'difference between the physical possibilities of young girls and the difficulties of the exercises has become dangerous.' These related issues confront gymnastics with its most grave problems in the 1980s. Unless the International Federation succeeds in breaking this tendency, women's gymnastics runs the risk of becoming the province of freaks, something which would be a profound disappointment to those who remember the sport as it has been, can be and hopefully will be again. The International Federation may, however, have difficulty in allaying or diverting the current development of the sport. Coaches and competitors will find ways to circumvent any restriction. In gymnastics, as in so many sports, the human desire to succeed is unconquerable and insatiable.

Appendix 1 Results of Olympics, World and European Championships

1896 Olympics, Athens, Greece

Men

Team Event – not held over combined exercises, but Germany won the team events for parallel bars and horizontal bars

High Bar
1. Hermann Weingartner, Germany
2. Alfred Flatov, Germany
3. Petmesas, Greece

Parallel Bars
1. Alfred Flatov, Germany
2. Hermann Weingartner, Germany
3. Louis Zutter, Switzerland

Pommel Horse
1. Louis Zutter, Switzerland
2. Hermann Weingartner, Germany
3. Gyula Kokas, Hungary

Vault
1. Karl Schumann, Germany
2. Louis Zutter, Switzerland

Rings
1. Joannis Mitropoulos, Greece
2. Hermann Weingartner, Germany
3. Petros Persakis, Greece

1900 Olympics, Paris, France

Men

Combined Exercises
1. Gustave Sandras, France, 302.00
2. Noël Bas, France, 295.00
3. Lucien Demanet, France, 293.00

1903 World Championships, Antwerp, Belgium

Men

Combined Exercises
1. J. Martinez, France, 122.00
2. equal: Jos Lux, France, 121.50
         G. Wiernickx, Belgium, 121.50

Team Event
1. France, 1044.00
2. Belgium, 981.00
3. Luxembourg, 909.00

High Bar
1. equal: J. Martinez, France, 20.50
         N. Pissie, France, 20.50
3. equal: N. Lecoutre, France, 20.00
         Van Hulle, Belgium, 20.00

Parallel Bars
1. equal: J. Martinez, France, 20.00
         F. Hentges, Luxembourg, 20.00
3. equal: E. Dua, Belgium, 19. 50
         N. Bordang, Luxembourg, 19.50

Vault
1. equal: N. Dejaeghere, France, 18.00
         Jos Lux, France, 18.00
         N. Thysen, Holland, 18.00

Rings
1. equal: J. Martinez, France, 20.00
         Jos Lux, Luxembourg, 20.00
3. N. Walravens, Belgium, 19.00

1904 Olympics, St Louis, United States

Men

Combined Exercises
1. Julius Lenhart, Austria, 69.80
2. Wilhelm Weber, Germany, 69.10
3. Adolf Spinnler, Switzerland, 67.99

Team Event
1. Turngemeinde Philadelphia, US, 374.43
2. New Yorker, US, 356.37
3. Central Chicago, US, 349.69

High Bar
1. equal: Anton Heida, US, 40.00
         Edward Henning, US, 40.00
3. George Eyser, US, 39.00

Parallel Bars
1. George Eyser, US, 44.00
2. Anton Heida, US, 43.00
3. John Duha, US, 40.00

Pommel Horse
1. Anton Heida, US, 42.00
2. George Eyser, US, 33.00
3. William Mertz, US, 29.00

Vault
1. equal: Anton Heida, US, 36.00
           George Eyser, US, 36.00
3. William Mertz, US, 31.00

Rings
1. Hermann Glass, US, 45.00
2. William Mertz, US, 35.00
3. Emil Voigt, US, 32.00

1905 World Championships, Bordeaux, France

Men

Combined Exercises
1. M. Lalue, France, 185.50
2. N. Lavielle, France, 184.25
3. A. Demanet, France, 179.25

Team Event
1. France, 1075.50
2. Holland, 941.75
3. Belgium, 906.75

High Bar
1. M. Lalue, France, 36.00
2. J. Martinez, France, 35.75
3. equal: A. Demanet, France, 35.50
           N. Pausse, France, 35.50

Parallel Bars
1. equal: J. Martinez, France, 33.50
           M. Lalue, France, 33.50
3. N. Pausse, France, 32.75

Vault
1. N. Dejaeghere, France, 34.75
2. M. Lalue, France, 34.50
3. N. Lavielle, France, 33.75

1906 Intercalated Olympics, Athens, Greece

Men

Combined Exercises
1. Pierre Paysse, France, 116.00
2. Alberto Braglia, Italy, 115.00
3. Georges Charmoille, France, 113.00

Team Event
1. Norway, 19.00
2. Denmark, 18.00
3. Italy, 16.71

1907 World Championships, Prague, Czechoslovakia

Men

Combined Exercises
1. J. Cada, Czechoslovakia, 167.25
2. J. Rolland, France, 158.75
3. F. Erben, Czechoslovakia, 157.25

Team Event
1. Czechoslovakia, 951.25
2. France, 923.00
3. Belgium, 872.25

High Bar
1. equal: N. Charmoille, France,
           23.75
           F. Erben, Czechoslovakia,
           23.75
3. J. Rolland, France, 23.50

Parallel Bars
1. Jos Lux, France, 21.75
2. J. Cada, Czechoslovakia, 20.75
3. equal: F. Erben, Czechoslovakia,
           20.50
           L. Segura, France, 20.50

Vault
1. F. Erben, Czechoslovakia, 22.25
2. J. Rolland, France, 21.00
3. Ch Sal, Czechoslovakia, 20.75

1908 Olympics, London, England

Men

Combined Exercises
1. Alberto Braglia, Italy, 317.00
2. Walter Tysal, Britain, 312.00
3. Louis Segura, France, 297.00

Team Event (Swedish gymnastics)
1. Sweden, 438.00
2. Norway, 425.00
3. Finland, 405.00

1909 World Championships, Luxembourg

Men

Combined Exercises
1. M. Torres, France, 163.25
2. J. Cada, Czechoslovakia, 159.50
3. N. Coidelle, France, 158.75

Team Event
1. France, 950.50
2. Czechoslovakia, 940.50
3. Italy, 924.25

High Bar
1. equal: J. Martinez, France, 24.00
        J. Cada, Czechoslovakia, 24.00
        F. Erben, Czechoslovakia, 24.00
4. K. Fuks, Slovak, 23.75

Parallel Bars
1. J. Martinez, France, 24.00
2. A. Castille, France, 20.75
3. equal: J. Cada, Czechoslovakia, 23.75
        M. Torres, France, 23.75

Rings
1. equal: G. Romano, Italy, 23.75
        M. Torres, France, 23.75
3. equal: F. Erben, Czechoslovakia, 23.25
        A. Manzoncini, Italy, 23.25
        G. Zampori, Italy, 23.25

1911 World Championships, Turin, Italy

Men

Combined Exercises
1. F. Steiner, Czechoslovakia, 168.25
2. J. Cada, Czechoslovakia, 167.62
3. equal: K. Stary, Czechoslovakia, 167.00
        S. Svoboda, Czechoslovakia, 167.00

Team Event
1. Czechoslovakia, 975.00
2. France, 934.41
3. Italy, 899.86

High Bar
1. J. Cada, Czechoslovakia, 24.00
2. M. Torres, France, 23.75
3. equal: S. Svoboda, France, 23.25
        G. Romano, Italy, 23.25

Parallel Bars
1. G. Zampori, Italy, 24.00
2. D. Follacci, France, 23.75
3. equal: Steiner, Lecoutre, Costa, Labeu,
        Salvi, Vidmar, 23.50

Pommel Horse
1. O. Palazzi, Italy, 24.00
2. P. Salvi, Italy, 23.00
3. G. Zampori, Italy, 23.00

Rings
1. equal: F. Steiner, Czechoslovakia, 24.00
        D. Follacci, France, 24.00
        P. Bianchi, Italy, 24.00

1912 Olympics, Stockholm, Sweden

Men

Combined Exercises
1. Alberto Braglia, Italy, 135.00
2. Louis Segura, France, 132.50
3. Adolfo Tunesi, Italy, 113.50

Team Event (optional and free exercises)
1. Italy, 265.75
2. Hungary, 227.25
3. Britain, 184.50
(There were also a Swedish gymnastics event
won by Sweden and an optional exercises
event won by Norway)

1913 World Championships, Paris, France

Men

Combined Exercises
1. M. Torres, France, 142.00
2. K. Stary, Czechoslovakia, 141.50
3. J. Sykora, Czechoslovakia, 136.50

Team Event
1. Czechoslovakia, 804.50
2. France, 777.75
3. Italy, 772.25

Floor Exercises
1. equal: G. Zampori, Italy, 30.00
        V. Rabic, Slovak, 30.00
3. M. Torres, France, 29.75

High Bar
1. equal: J. Cada, Czechoslovakia, 20.00
   M. Torres, France, 20.00
   N. Aubry, France, 20.00
   Demol, Belgium, 20.00
   O. Palazzi, Italy, 20.00
6. J. Sykora, Czechoslovakia, 19.50

Parallel Bars
1. equal: G. Zampori, Italy, 20.00
   N. Boni, Italy, 20.00
3. P. Hentges, Luxembourg, 15.90

Pommel Horse
1. equal: G. Zampori, Italy, 19.75
   N. Aubry, France, 19.75
   O. Palazzi, Italy, 19.75
4. M. Torres, France, 19.75

Vault
1. equal: K. Stary, Czechoslovakia, 10.00
   B. Sadoun, France, 10.00
   O. Palazzi, Italy, 10.00
   S. Vidmar, Yugoslavia, 10.00

Rings
1. equal: N. Grech, France, 19.75
   M. Torres, France, 19.75
   G. Zampori, Italy, 19.75
   N. Boni, Italy, 19.75

1920 Olympics, Antwerp, Belgium

Men

Combined Exercises
1. Giorgio Zampori, Italy, 88.35
1. Marcel Torres, France, 87.62
3. Jean Gounot, France, 87.45

Team Event
1. Italy, 359.855
2. Belgium, 346.785
3. France, 240.100
(There were also a Swedish gymnastics event won by Sweden and an optional exercises event won by Denmark)

1922 World Championships, Ljubljana, Yugoslavia

Men

Combined Exercises
1. equal: P. Sumi, Yugoslavia, 135.25
   F. Pechacek, Czechoslovakia, 135.25
3. S. Derganc, Yugoslavia, 135.15

Team Event
1. Czechoslovakia, 773.00
2. Yugoslavia, 764.00
3. France, 636.00

High Bar
1. equal: M. Klinger, Czechoslovakia, 19.75
   L. Stukelj, Yugoslavia, 19.75
   P. Sumi, Yugoslavia, 19.75

Parallel Bars
1. equal: L. Stukelj, Yugoslavia, 20.00
   S. Derganc, Yugoslavia, 20.00
   N. Jindrich, Czechoslovakia, 20.00
   M. Klinger, Czechoslovakia, 20.00
   V. Simoncic, Yugoslavia, 20.00

Pommel Horse
1. equal: M. Klinger, Czechoslovakia, 19.25
   N. Jindrich, Czechoslovakia, 19.25
   L. Stukelj, Yugoslavia, 19.25

Rings
1. equal: N. Karasek, Czechoslovakia, 19.75
   N. Maly, Czechoslovakia, 19.75
   L. Stukelj, Yugoslavia, 19.75
   P. Sumi, Yugoslavia, 19.75

1924 Olympics, Paris, France

Men

Combined Exercises
1. Leon Stukelj, Yugoslavia, 110.340
2. Robert Prazak, Czechoslovakia, 110.323
3. Bedrich Supcik, Czechoslovakia, 106.930

Team Event
1. Italy, 838.058
2. France, 820.528
3. Switzerland, 816.660

High Bar
1. Leon Stukelj, Yugoslavia, 19.730
2. Jean Gutweniger, Switzerland, 19.236
3. A. Higelin, France, 19.163

Parallel Bars
1. August Guttinger, Switzerland, 21.63
2. Robert Prazak, Czechoslovakia, 21.61
3. Giorgio Zampori, Italy, 21.45

Pommel Horse
1. Josef Wilhelm, Switzerland, 21.23
2. Jean Gutweniger, Switzerland, 21.13
3. Antoine Rebetez, Switzerland, 20.73

Vault
1. Frank Kriz, US, 9.98
2. Jan Koutny, Czechoslovakia, 9.97
3. Bohumil Morkovsky, Czechoslovakia, 9.93

Rings
1. Francesco Martino, Italy, 21.553
2. Robert Prazak, Czechoslovakia, 21.483
3. Ladislav Vacha, Czechoslovakia, 21.430

1926 World Championships, Lyon, France

Men

Combined Exercises
1. P. Sumi, Yugoslavia, 168.550
2. J. Effenberger, Czechoslovakia, 166.288
3. L. Vacha, Czechoslovakia, 165.946

Team Event
1. Czechoslovakia, 1198.797
2. Yugoslavia, 1162.867
3. France, 1152.230

High Bar
1. L. Stukelj, Yugoslavia, 31.60
2. J. Primozic, Yugoslavia, 31.55
3. L. Vacha, Czechoslovakia, 31.35

Parallel Bars
1. L. Vacha, Czechoslovakia, 31.25
2. J. Gajdos, Czechoslovakia, 30.60
3. L. Stukelj, Yugoslavia, 30.45

Pommel Horse
1. N. Karafiat, Czechoslovakia, 30.90
2. J. Gajdos, Czechoslovakia, 30.85
3. L. Vacha, Czechoslovakia, 30.80

Rings
1. L. Stukelj, Yugoslavia, 31.85
2. L. Vacha, Czechoslovakia, 31.75
3. B. Supcik, Czechoslovakia, 31.55

1928 Olympics, Amsterdam, Holland

Men

Combined Exercises
1. Georges Miesz, Switzerland, 247.625
2. Hermann Hanggi, Switzerland, 246.625
3. Leon Stukelj, Yugoslavia, 244.875

Team Event
1. Switzerland, 1718.625
2. Czechoslovakia, 1712.5
3. Yugoslavia, 1648.5

High Bar
1. Georges Miesz, Switzerland, 19.17
2. Romeo Neri, Italy, 19.00
3. Eugène Mack, Switzerland, 18.92

Parallel Bars
1. Ladislav Vacha, Czechoslovakia, 18.83
2. Josip Primozic, Yugoslavia, 18.50
3. Hermann Hanggi, Switzerland, 18.08

Pommel Horse
1. Hermann Hanggi, Switzerland, 19.75
2. Georges Miesz, Switzerland, 19.25
3. Heikki Savolainen, Finland, 18.83

Vault
1. Eugène Mack, Switzerland, 9.58
2. E. Loffler, Czechoslovakia, 9.50
3. Stane Derganc, Yugoslavia, 9.46

Rings
1. Leon Stukelj, Yugoslavia, 19.25
2. Ladislav Vacha, Czechoslovakia, 19.17
3. E. Loffler, Czechoslovakia, 18.83

Women

Team Event
1. Holland, 316.75
2. Italy, 289.00
3. Britain, 258.25

1930 World Championships, Luxembourg

Men

Combined Exercises
1. J. Primozic, Yugoslavia, 152.45
2. J. Gajdos, Czechoslovakia, 150.55
3. E. Loffler, Czechoslovakia, 148.65

Team Event
1. Czechoslovakia, 897.30
2. France, 871.75
3. Yugoslavia, 849.75

Floor Exercises
1. J. Primozic, Yugoslavia
2. E. Loffler, Czechoslovakia
3. A. Krauss, France

High Bar
1. E. Pelle, Hungary
2. N. Peter, Hungary
3. L. Stukelj, Yugoslavia

Parallel Bars
1. J. Primozic, Yugoslavia
2. A. Krauss, France
3. L. Vacha, Czechoslovakia

Pommel Horse
1. J. Primozic, Yugoslavia
2. P. Sumi, Yugoslavia
3. J. Gajdos, Czechoslovakia

Rings
1. E. Loffler, Czechoslovakia
2. B. Supcik, Czechoslovakia
3. J. Gajdos, Czechoslovakia

1932 Olympics, Los Angeles, United States

Men

Combined Exercises
1. Romeo Neri, Italy, 140.625
2. Istvan Pelle, Hungary, 134.925
3. Heikki Savolainen, Finland, 134.575

Team Event
1. Italy, 541.850
2. United States, 522.275
3. Finland, 509.995

Floor Exercises
1. Istvan Pelle, Hungary, 28.80
2. Georges Miesz, Switzerland, 28.40
3. Mario Lertora, Italy, 27.70

High Bar
1. Dallas Bixler, US, 18.33
2. Heikki Savolainen, Finland, 18.07
3. Einari Teraesvirta, Finland, 18.07

Parallel Bars
1. Romeo Neri, Italy, 18.97
2. Istvan Pelle, Hungary, 18.60
3. Heikki Savolainen, Finland, 18.27

Pommel Horse
1. Istvan Pelle, Hungary, 19.07
2. Omero Bonoli, Italy, 18.87
3. Frank Haubold, US, 18.57

Vault
1. Savino Guglielmetti, Italy, 18.03
2. Alfred Jochim, Germany, 17.77
3. Edward Carmichael, US, 17.53

Rings
1. George Gulack, US, 18.97
2. William Denton, US, 18.60
3. Giovanni Lattuada, Italy, 18.50

1934 World Championships, Budapest, Hungary

Men

Combined Exercises
1. E. Mack, Switzerland, 138.95
2. R. Neri, Italy, 137.75
3. E. Loffler, Czechoslovakia, 136.15

Floor Exercises
1. G. Miesz, Switzerland, 18.95
2. E. Mack, Switzerland, 18.35
3. N. Krotsch, Germany, 18.25

High Bar
1. Winter, Germany, 19.65
2. equal: Sandrock, Germany, 19.45
　　　　　G. Miesz, Switzerland, 19.45

Parallel Bars
1. E. Mack, Switzerland, 19.75
2. J. Walter, Switzerland, 19.25
3. W. Bach, Switzerland, 19.20

Pommel Horse
1. E. Mack, Switzerland, 19.25
2. E. Steinemann, Switzerland, 18.90
3. J. Sladek, Czechoslovakia, 18.75

Vault
1. E. Mack, Switzerland, 20.00
2. E. Steinemann, Switzerland, 19.40
3. R. Neri, Italy, 19.20

Rings
1. A. Hudec, Czechoslovakia, 19.45
2. E. Mack, Switzerland, 19.00
3. equal: N. Logelin, Luxembourg, 18.90
　　　　　J. Kolinger, Czechoslovakia, 18.90

Women

Combined Exercises
1. V. Dekanova, Czechoslovakia, 60.28
2. N. Koloczy, Hungary, 59.58
3. N. Skyrlinska, Poland, 58.65

Team Event
1. Czechoslovakia, 738.06
2. Hungary, 734.40
3. Poland, 629.48

1936 Olympics, Berlin, Germany

Men

Combined Exercises
1. Karl Schwarzmann, Germany, 113.100
2. Eugène Mack, Switzerland, 112.334
3. Konrad Frey, Germany, 111.532

Team Event
1. Germany, 657.430
2. Switzerland, 654.802
3. Finland, 638.468

Floor Exercises
1. Georges Miesz, Switzerland, 19.166
2. Josef Walter, Switzerland, 18.500
3. equal: Konrad Frey, Germany, 18.466
         Eugène Mack, Switzerland, 18.466

High Bar
1. Aleksanteri Saarvala, Finland, 19.433
2. Konrad Frey, Germany, 19.267
3. Karl Schwarzmann, Germany, 19.233

Parallel Bars
1. Konrad Frey, Germany, 19.067
2. Michael Reusch, Switzerland, 19.034
3. Karl Schwarzmann, Germany, 18.967

Pommel Horse
1. Konrad Frey, Germany, 19.333
2. Eugène Mack, Switzerland, 19.167
3. Albert Bachmann, Switzerland, 19.067

Vault
1. Karl Schwarzmann, Germany, 19.200
2. Eugène Mack, Switzerland, 18.967
3. Matthias Volz, Germany, 18.467

Rings
1. Alois Hudec, Czechoslovakia, 19.433
2. Leon Stukelj, Yugoslavia, 18.870
3. Matthias Volz, Germany, 18.670

Women

Team Event
1. Germany, 506.50
2. Czechoslovakia, 503.50
3. Hungary, 499.00

1938 World Championships, Prague, Czechoslovakia

Men

Combined Exercises
1. J. Gajdos, Czechoslovakia, 138.066
2. J. Sladek, Czechoslovakia, 137.466
3. E. Mack, Switzerland, 136.400

Team Event
1. Czechoslovakia, 806.83
2. Switzerland, 791.20
3. Yugoslavia, 741.26

Floor Exercises
1. J. Gajdos, Czechoslovakia, 18.833
2. equal: E. Mack, Switzerland, 18.566
         A. Hudec, Czechoslovakia, 18.566

High Bar
1. M. Reusch, Switzerland, 19.766
2. A. Hudec, Czechoslovakia, 19.700
3. W. Beck, Switzerland, 19.432

Parallel Bars
1. M. Reusch, Switzerland, 19.563
2. A. Hudec, Czechoslovakia, 19.553
3. J. Primozic, Yugoslavia, 18.733

Pommel Horse
1. equal: M. Reusch, Switzerland, 19.566
         V. Petracek, Czechoslovakia, 19.466
3. L. Schurmann, Switzerland, 19.400

Vault
1. E. Mack, Switzerland, 19.83
2. W. Beck, Switzerland, 19.66
3. H. Nagelin, Switzerland, 19.50

Rings
1. A. Hudec, Czechoslovakia, 19.633
2. M. Reusch, Switzerland, 19.300
3. V. Petracek, Czechoslovakia, 18.773

Women

Combined Exercises
1. V. Dekanova, Czechoslovakia, 83.66
2. Z. Vjerzimirskova, Czechoslovakia, 82.71
3. M. Palfyeva, Czechoslovakia, 81.98

Team Event
1. Czechoslovakia, 552.76
2. Yugoslavia, 513.96
3. Poland, 510.21

Parallel Bars
1. V. Dekanova, Czechoslovakia, 14.85
2. equal: V. Folotova, Czechoslovakia, 14.80
        B. Dobesova, Czechoslovakia, 14.80

Vault
1. equal: M. Palfyeva, Czechoslovakia, 14.83
        N. Majovska, Poland, 14.83
3. equal: M. Sket, Yugoslavia, 14.70
        V. Dekanova, Czechoslovakia, 14.70
        B. Dobesova, Czechoslovakia, 14.70

Beam
1. V. Dekanova, Czechoslovakia, 14.90
2. M. Sket, Yugoslavia, 14.75
3. M. Palfyeva, Czechoslovakia, 14.70

Floor Exercises
1. M. Palfyeva, Czechoslovakia, 9.95
2. Z. Vjerzimirskovska, Czechoslovakia, 9.90
3. equal: V. Folotova, Czechoslovakia, 9.80
        V. Noskiewicz, Poland, 9.80

1948 Olympics, London, England

Men

Combined Exercises
1. V. Huhtanen, Finland, 229.70
2. W. Lehmann, Switzerland, 229.00
3. P. Aaltonen, Finland, 228.80
4. J. Stalder, Switzerland, 228.70
5. C. Kipfer, Switzerland, 227.10
Other placings:
44. E. Scrobe, US, 213.90
49. V. Autorio, US, 211.30
53. W. Roetzheim, US, 209.10
55. J. Kotys, US, 208.50
60. G. Weedon, Britain, 205.60
62. F. Cumiskey, US, 205.15
63. R. Sorensen, US, 204.55
67. F. Turner, Britain, 202.60
69. W. Bonsall, US, 201.70
79. K. Buffin, Britain, 188.65
83. A. Wales, Britain, 180.80
92. P. May, Britain, 171.45
98. J. Flaherty, Britain, 165.30

Team Event
1. Finland, 1358.30
2. Switzerland, 1356.70
3. Hungary, 1330.85
4. France, 1315.00
5. Italy, 1300.30
6. Czechoslovakia, 1251.30

7. United States, 1245.40
8. Denmark, 1212.15
Other placings:
12. Britain, 1057.95

Floor Exercises
1. F. Pataki, Hungary, 38.70
2. J. Mogyorossy Klencs, Hungary, 38.40
3. Z. Ruzicka, Czechoslovakia, 38.10
4. R. Dot, France, 37.80
5. T. Gronne, Denmark, 37.65

High Bar
1. J. Stalder, Switzerland, 39.70
2. W. Lehmann, Switzerland, 39.40
3. V. Huhtanen, Finland, 39.20
4. equal: A. Saarvala, Finland, 38.80
        E. Studer, Switzerland, 38.80
        L. Santha, Hungary, 38.80
        R. Dot, France, 38.80

Parallel Bars
1. M. Reusch, Switzerland, 39.50
2. V. Huhtanen, Finland, 39.30
3. equal: J. Stalder, Switzerland, 39.10
        C. Kipfer, Switzerland, 39.10
5. W. Lehmann, Switzerland, 39.00

Pommel Horse
1. equal: V. Huhtanen, Finland, 38.70
        P. Aaltonen, Finland, 38.70
        H. Savolainen, Finland, 38.70
4. L. Zanetti, Italy, 38.30
5. G. Figone, Italy, 38.20

Vault
1. P. Aaltonen, Finland, 39.10
2. O. Rove, Finland, 39.00
3. equal: F. Pataki, Hungary, 38.50
        J. Mogyorossy Klencs, Hungary, 38.50
        L. Sotornik, Czechoslovakia, 38.50

Rings
1. K. Frei, Switzerland, 39.60
2. M. Reusch, Switzerland, 39.10
3. Z. Ruzicka, Czechoslovakia, 38.50
4. W. Lehmann, Switzerland, 38.40
5. equal: J. Stalder, Switzerland, 38.30
        E. Studer, Switzerland, 38.30

Women

Team Event
1. Czechoslovakia, 445.45
2. Hungary, 440.55

3. US, 422.60
4. Sweden, 417.95
5. Holland, 408.35
6. Austria, 405.45
7. Yugoslavia, 397.90
8. Italy, 394.20
9. Britain, 392.95

1950 World Championships, Basle, Switzerland

Men

Combined Exercises
1. Walter Lehmann, Switzerland, 143.30
2. Marcel Adatta, Switzerland, 141.00
3. Olavi Rove, Finland, 140.80
4. Guido Figone, Italy, 139.95
5. Josef Stoffel, Luxembourg, 139.50
Other placings :
49. Frank Turner, Britain, 100.95

Team Event
1. Switzerland, 852.25
2. Finland, 838.50
3. France, 807.85
4. Italy, 728.90
5. Yugoslavia, 664.90
6. Egypt, 623.80

Floor Exercises
1. Josef Stalder, Switzerland, 19.35
2. Ernst Gebendinger, Switzerland, 19.25
3. Raymond Dot, France, 19.20
4. equal: Kaino Lempinen, Finland, 19.15
    Olavi Rove, Finland, 19.15
    E. Wister, Austria, 19.15

High Bar
1. Paavo Aaltonen, Finland, 19.45
2. Vaikko Huthanen, Finland, 19.40
3. equal: Walter Lehmann, Switzerland, 19.35
    Josef Stalder, Switzerland, 19.35
5. Olavi Rove, Finland, 19.25

Parallel Bars
1. Hans Eugster, Switzerland, 19.85
2. Olavi Rove, Finland, 19.45
3. Raymond Dot, France, 19.35
4. Walter Lehmann, Switzerland, 19.30
5. Heikki Savolainen, Finland, 19.25

Pommel Horse
1. Josef Stalder, Switzerland, 19.70
2. Marcel Adatte, Switzerland, 19.35
3. Walter Lehmann, Switzerland, 19.05
4. equal: Veikako Huthanen, Finland, 18.90
    Melchior Thalmann, Switzerland, 18.90

Vault
1. Ernst Gebendinger, Switzerland, 19.45
2. Olavi Rove, Finland, 19.35
3. Walter Lehmann, Switzerland, 19.30
4. Josef Stalder, Switzerland, 19.20
5. Melchior Thalmann, Switzerland, 19.20

Rings
1. Walter Lehmann, Switzerland, 19.60
2. Olavi Rove, Finland, 19.30
3. Hans Eugster, Switzerland, 19.20
4. Ali Zaki, Egypt, 19.15
5. Guido Figone, Italy, 18.90

Women

Combined Exercises
1. Rakoczy, Poland, 94.016
2. Peterson, Switzerland, 91.700
3. Kolar, Austria, 91.000
4. Bergren, Sweden, 90.633
5. Lemoine, France, 90.516

Team Event
1. Sweden, 607.500
2. France, 598.766
3. Italy, 594.250
4. Yugoslavia, 589.333
5. Poland, 587.333
6. Austria, 585.783
7. Belgium, 509.866

Vault
1. Rakoczy, Poland, 23.566
2. Kolar, Austria, 23.466
3. Lemoine, France, 23.400
4. Lindberg, Sweden, 23.366
5. Reindlowa, Poland, 23.300

Beam
1. Rakoczy, Poland, 23.433
2. Nutti, Italy, 23.330
3. Macchini, Italy, 23.200
4. Reindlowa, Poland, 22.966
5. Jouffroy, France, 22.933

Floor Exercises
1. Rakoczy, Poland, 23.166
2. Kocis, Yugoslavia, 23.033
3. Reindlowa, Poland, 23.000
4. Jouffroy, France, 22.966
5. Michelis, Italy, 22.600

Asymmetric Bars
1. equal: Kolar, Austria, 24.00
       Petersen, Sweden, 24.00
3. Rakoczy, Poland, 23.85
4. Sandahl, Sweden, 23.60
5. Schramm, Austria, 23.55

1952 Olympics, Helsinki, Finland

Men

Combined Exercises
1. Viktor Chukarin, Soviet Union, 115.70
2. Grant Chaguinjan, Soviet Union, 114.96
3. Josef Stalder, Switzerland, 114.75
4. Valentin Mouratov, Soviet Union, 113.65
5. Hans Eugster, Switzerland, 113.40
Other placings:
30. Edward Scrobe, US, 110.40
34. Robert Stout, US, 110.15
59. William Roetzheim, US, 107.05
73. Frank Turner, Britain, 104.70
80. Donald Holder, US, 103.50
81. John Beckner, US, 103.40
89. Charles Simms, US, 102.40
90. Walter Blattmann, US, 102.35
98. John Whitford, Britain, 101.65

Team Event
1. Soviet Union, 574.35
2. Switzerland, 567.50
3. Finland, 564.20
4. Germany, 561.20
5. Japan, 556.90
6. Hungary, 555.80
7. Czechoslovakia, 555.55
8. United States, 543.15
Other placings:
21. Britain, 490.50

Floor Exercises
1. Karl Thoresson, Sweden, 19.25
2. equal: Tadao Uesako, Japan, 19.15
       Jerzy Jokiel, Poland, 19.15
4. Takashi Ono, Japan, 19.05
5. Onni Lappalainen, Finland, 19.00

High Bar
1. Jack Gunthard, Switzerland, 19.55
2. equal: Josef Stalder, Switzerland, 19.50
       Alfred Schwarzmann, Germany, 19.50
4. equal: Heikki Savolainen, Finland, 19.45
       Viktor Chukarin, Soviet Union, 19.40

Parallel Bars
1. Hans Eugster, Switzerland, 19.65
2. Viktor Chukarin, Soviet Union, 19.60
3. Josef Stalder, Switzerland, 19.50
4. Grant Chaguinjan, Soviet Union, 19.35
5. equal: Eugen Korolkov, Soviet Union, 19.30
       Jean Tschabold, Switzerland, 19.30

Pommel Horse
1. Viktor Chukarin, Soviet Union, 19.50
2. equal: Grant Chaguinjan, Soviet Union, 19.40
       Eugen Korolkov, Soviet Union, 19.40
4. Mikhail Perelman, Soviet Union, 19.30
5. Josef Stalder, Switzerland, 19.20

Vault
1. Viktor Chukarin, Soviet Union, 19.20
2. Masao Takemoto, Japan, 19.15
3. equal: Takashi Ono, Japan, 19.10
       Tadao Uesako, Japan, 19.10
5. equal: Hans Eugster, Switzerland, 18.95
       Theo Wied, Germany, 18.95

Rings
1. Grant Chaguinjan, Soviet Union, 19.75
2. Viktor Chukarin, Soviet Union, 19.55
3. equal: Hans Eugster, Switzerland, 19.40
       Dimitri Leonkin, Soviet Union, 19.40
5. Valentin Mouratov, Soviet Union, 19.35

Women

Combined Exercises
1. Maria Gorokhovskaya, Soviet Union, 76.78
2. Nina Botsharova, Soviet Union, 75.94
3. Margit Korondi, Hungary, 75.82
4. Galina Minaitsheva, Soviet Union, 75.67
5. Galina Urbanovitch, Soviet Union, 75.64
Other placings:
64. Marion Barone, US, 69.30
65. Ruth Grulkowski, US, 69.28

73. Clare Lomady, US, 68.38
78. Gwynedd Lewis, Britain, 68.01
83. Ruth Topalian, US, 67.81
89. Pat Hirst, Britain, 67.21

Beam
1. Mina Botsharova, Soviet Union, 19.22
2. Maria Gorokhovskaya, Soviet Union, 19.13
3. Margit Korondi, Hungary, 19.02
4. Agnes Keleti, Hungary, 18.96
5. Galina Urbanovitch, Soviet Union, 18.93

Floor Exercises
1. Agnes Keleti, Hungary, 19.36
2. Maria Gorokhovskaya, Soviet Union, 19.20
3. Margit Korondi, Hungary, 19.00
4. equal : Galina Urbanovitch, Soviet Union, 18.99
   Karolyne Gulyas, Hungary, 18.99

Vault
1. Ekaterina Kalintshuk, Soviet Union, 19.20
2. Maria Gorokhovskaya, Soviet Union, 19.19
3. Galina Minaitsheva, Soviet Union, 19.16
4. Medeja Dsugeli, Soviet Union, 19.13
5. Galina Urbanovitch, Soviet Union, 19.10

Asymmetric Bars
1. Margit Korondi, Hungary, 19.49
2. Maria Gorokhovskaya, Soviet Union, 19.20
3. Agnes Keleti, Hungary, 19.16
4. equal : Mina Botsharova, Soviet Union, 18.99
   Pelageya Danilova, Soviet Union, 18.99

1954 World Championships, Rome, Italy

Men

Combined Exercises
1. equal : Viktor Chukarin, Soviet Union, 115.45
   Valentin Mouratov, Soviet Union, 115.45
3. Grant Chaguinjan, Soviet Union, 114.60
4. equal : Boris Shaklin, Soviet Union, 114.05
   Albert Azarian, Soviet Union, 114.05

Other placings :
89. Charles Simms, US, 98.40

Team Event
1. Soviet Union, 689.90
2. Japan, 673.25
3. Switzerland, 671.55
4. Germany, 670.25
5. Czechoslovakia, 661.40
6. Finland, 659.85
7. Hungary, 650.00
8. Italy, 637.45

Floor Exercises
1. equal : Valentin Mouratov, Soviet Union, 19.25
   Masao Takemoto, Japan, 19.25
3. William Thoresson, Sweden, 19.20
4. equal : Victor Chukarin, Soviet Union, 19.15
   Masami Kubota, Japan, 19.15

High Bar
1. Valentin Mouratov, Soviet Union, 19.70
2. equal : Helmut Bantz, Germany, 19.40
   Boris Shaklin, Soviet Union, 19.40
4. Joseph Stalder, Switzerland, 19.30
5. Masao Takemoto, Japan, 19.25

Parallel Bars
1. Victor Chukarin, Soviet Union, 19.60
2. Joseph Stalder, Switzerland, 19.55
3. equal : Masao Takemoto, Japan, 19.40
   Hans Eugster, Switzerland, 19.40
   Helmut Bantz, Germany, 19.40

Pommel Horse
1. Grant Chaguinjan, Soviet Union, 19.30
2. Joseph Stalder, Switzerland, 19.25
3. Victor Chukarin, Soviet Union, 19.20
4. Boris Shaklin, Soviet Union, 19.15
5. Ivan Vostrikov Soviet Union, 18.90

Vault
1. Leo Sotornik, Czechoslovakia, 19.25
2. Helmut Bantz, Germany, 19.20
3. Sergei Diaiani, Soviet Union, 19.10
4. equal : Albert Azarian, Soviet Union, 18.90
   Takashi Ono, Japan, 18.90

Rings
1. Albert Azarian, Soviet Union, 19.75
2. Eugene Korolkov, Soviet Union, 19.55
3. Valentin Mouratov, Soviet Union, 19.50
4. Victor Chukarin, Soviet Union, 19.45
5. Grant Chaguinjan, Soviet Union, 19.40

Women

Combined Exercises
1. Galina Roudiko, Soviet Union, 75.68

2. Eva Bosakova, Czechoslovakia, 75.11
3. Helena Rakoczy, Poland, 74.37
4. Editz Perenyi, Hungary, 74.31
5. Elena Leusteann, Romania, 74.24

Team Event
1. Soviet Union, 524.31
2. Hungary, 518.28
3. Czechoslovakia, 511.75
4. Romania, 498.57
5. Italy, 495.77
6. Poland, 495.66
7. Bulgaria, 494.03
8. Sweden, 491.21

Vault
1. equal: Tamara Manina, Soviet Union, 18.96
         Anna Petersson, Sweden, 18.96
3. Evy Bergren, Sweden, 18.93
4. Maria Gorokhovskaya, Soviet Union, 18.86
5. Galina Roudiko, Soviet Union, 18.79

Beam
1. Keiko Tanaka, Japan, 18.89
2. Eva Bosakova, Czechoslovakia, 18.76
3. Agnes Keleti, Hungary, 18.72
4. Edith Perenyi, Hungary, 18.66
5. Galina Roudiko, Soviet Union, 18.60

Floor Exercises
1. Tamara Manina, Soviet Union, 19.39
2. Eva Bosakova, Czechoslovakia, 19.16
3. Maria Gorokhovskaya, Soviet Union, 19.12
4. Agnes Keleti, Hungary, 19.10
5. Galina Roudiko, Soviet Union, 18.96

Asymmetric Bars
1. Agnes Keleti, Hungary, 19.46
2. Galina Roudiko, Soviet Union, 19.33
3. Helena Rakoczy, Poland, 19.20
4. equal: Nina Botcharova, Soviet Union, 19.13
         Eva Bosakova, Czechoslovakia, 19.13

1955 European Championships, Frankfurt, West Germany

Men

Combined Exercises
1. Boris Shaklin, Soviet Union, 57.80
2. Albert Azarian, Soviet Union, 56.75
3. Helmut Bantz, Germany, 56.65

Floor Exercises
1. Vladimir Prorok, Czechoslovakia, 9.75
2. Jan Cronstedt, Sweden, 9.70
3. equal: Adalbert Dickhunt, Germany, 9.60
         Mincso Todorov, Hungary, 9.60

High Bar
1. Boris Shaklin, Soviet Union, 9.75
2. equal: Albert Azarian, Soviet Union, 9.60
         Jan Cronstedt, Sweden, 9.60

Parallel Bars
1. equal: Albert Azarian, Soviet Union, 9.75
         Helmut Bantz, Germany 9.75
         Boris Shaklin, Soviet Union, 9.75

Pommel Horse
1. Boris Shaklin, Soviet Union, 9.75
2. Jan Cronstedt, Sweden, 9.35
3. Hans Sauter, Switzerland, 9.30

Vault
1. Adalbert Dickhunt, Germany, 9.75
2. equal: Helmut Bantz, Germany, 9.60
         Joseph Stoffel, Switzerland, 9.60

Rings
1. Albert Azarian, Soviet Union, 9.85
2. equal: Helmut Bantz, Germany, 9.55
         Vladimir Prorok, Czechoslovakia, 9.55
         Boris Shaklin, Soviet Union, 9.55

1956 Olympics, Melbourne, Australia

Men

Combined Exercises
1. Viktor Chukarin, Soviet Union, 114.25
2. Takashi Ono, Japan, 114.20
3. Yuri Titov, Soviet Union, 113.80
4. Masao Takemoto, Japan, 113.55
5. Valentin Mouratov, Soviet Union, 113.30
Other placings:
17. John Beckner, US, 111.00
31. Armando Vega, US, 108.45
32. Charles Simms, US, 108.40
35. Richard Beckner, US, 108.30
38. Nik Stuart, Britain, 107.85
39. Abie Grossfeld, US, 107.75
43. William Tom, US, 107.35
50. Frank Turner, Britain, 103.15

Team Event
1. Soviet Union, 568.25
2. Japan, 566.40

3. Finland, 555.95
4. Czechoslovakia, 554.10
5. Germany, 552.45
6. United States, 547.50
7. Australia, 477.15

Floor Exercises
1. Valentin Mouratov, Soviet Union, 19.20
2. equal: Viktor Chukarin, Soviet Union, 19.10
   William Thoresson, Sweden, 19.10
   Nobuyuki Aihara, Japan, 19.10
5. Yuri Titov, Soviet Union, 18.95

High Bar
1. Takashi Ono, Japan, 19.60
2. Yuri Titov, Soviet Union, 19.40
3. Masao Takemoto, Japan, 19.30
4. equal: Viktor Chukarin, Soviet Union, 19.25
   Pavel Stolbov, Soviet Union, 19.25

Parallel Bars
1. Viktor Chukarin, Soviet Union, 19.20
2. Masami Kubota, Japan, 19.15
3. equal: Masao Takemoto, Japan, 19.10
   Takashi Ono, Japan, 19.10
5. Albert Azarian, Soviet Union, 19.00

Pommel Horse
1. Boris Shaklin, Soviet Union, 19.25
2. Takashi Ono, Japan, 19.20
3. Viktor Chukarin, Soviet Union, 19.10
4. Josef Skvor, Czechoslovakia, 19.05
5. Yuri Titov, Soviet Union, 19.00

Vault
1. equal: Helmut Bantz, Germany, 18.85
   Valentin Mouratov, Soviet Union, 18.85
3. Yuri Titov, Soviet Union, 18.75
4. equal: Boris Shaklin, Soviet Union, 18.70
   Theo Wied, Germany, 18.70

Rings
1. Albert Azarian, Soviet Union, 19.35
2. Valentin Mouratov, Soviet Union, 19.15
3. equal: Masami Kubota, Japan, 19.10
   Masao Takemoto, Japan, 19.10
5. equal: Takashi Ono, Japan, 19.05
   Nobuyuki Aihara, Japan, 19.05

Women

Combined Exercises
1. Larissa Latynina, Soviet Union, 74.933

2. Agnes Keleti, Hungary, 74.633
3. Sofia Mouratova, Soviet Union, 74.466
4. equal: Olga Tass, Hungary, 74.366
   Elena Leusteanu, Romania, 74.366

Other placings :
51. Sandra Ruddick, US, 69.133
52. Muriel Davis, US, 68.933
54. Joyce Racek, US, 68.500
55. Jacqueline Klein, US, 68.300
57. Doris Fuchs, US, 67.733
58. Judy Howe, US, 67.200
60. Pat Hirst, Britain, 65.833

Team Event
1. Soviet Union, 444.800
2. Hungary, 443.500
3. Romania, 438.200
4. Poland, 436.500
5. Czechoslovakia, 435.366
6. Japan, 433.666
7. Italy, 428.666
8. Sweden, 428.600
9. United States, 413.200

Vault
1. Larissa Latynina, Soviet Union, 18.833
2. Tamara Manina, Soviet Union, 18.799
3. equal: Olga Tass, Hungary, 18.733
   Ann Sofi Volling, Sweden, 18.733
5. Sofia Mouratova, Soviet Union, 18.666

Beam
1. Agnes Keleti, Hungary, 18.799
2. equal: Tamara Manina, Soviet Union, 18.633
   Eva Bosakova, Czechoslovakia, 18.633
4. equal: Anna Marjekova, Czechoslovakia, 18.533
   Larissa Latynina, Soviet Union, 18.533

Floor Exercises
1. equal: Agnes Keleti, Hungary, 18.732
   Larissa Latynina, Soviet Union, 18.732
3. Elena Leusteanu, Romania, 18.700
4. equal: Sofia Mouratova, Soviet Union, 18.566
   Keiko Tanaka, Japan, 18.566
   Eva Bosakova, Czechoslovakia, 18.566

Asymmetric Bars
1. Agnes Keleti, Hungary, 18.966
2. Larissa Latynina, Soviet Union, 18.833
3. Sofia Muratova, Soviet Union, 18.800
4. Eva Bosakova, Czechoslovakia, 18.733
5. Helena Rakoczy, Poland, 18.700

1957 European Championships

Paris, France

Men

Combined Exercises

1. Jo Blume, Spain, 57.40
2. Yuri Titov, Soviet Union, 56.85
3. Max Benker, Switzerland, 55.90

Floor Exercises
1. William Thoresson, Sweden, 19.55
2. Nik Stuart, Britain, 19.20
3. Herbert Schmitt, West Germany, 19.10

High Bar
1. Jack Gunthard, Switzerland, 19.55
2. Jo Blume, Spain, 19.45
3. Yuri Titov, Soviet Union, 19.20

Parallel Bars
1. equal: Jack Gunthard, Switzerland,
    19.15
    Jo Blume, Spain, 19.15
3. Max Benker, Switzerland, 19.10

Pommel Horse
1. Jo Blume, Spain, 19.20
2. Max Benker, Switzerland, 19.00
3. Ivan Caklec, Yugoslavia, 18.60

Vault
1. Yuri Titov, Soviet Union, 19.15
2. Raymond Csanyi, Hungary, 18.85
3. William Thoresson, Sweden, 18.80

Rings
1. Jo Blume, Spain, 19.65
2. Yuri Titov, Soviet Union, 19.55
3. Kalevi Suomeni, Finland, 19.45

Bucharest, Romania

Women

Combined Exercises
1. Larissa Latynina, Soviet Union, 38.645
2. Elena Teodorescu, Romania, 37.798
3. Sonia Iovan, Romania, 37.399

Vault
1. Larissa Latynina, Soviet Union, 19.229
2. Tamara Manina, Soviet Union, 18.933
3. Sonia Iovan, Romania, 18.733

Beam
1. Larissa Latynina, Soviet Union, 19.000
2. Sonia Iovan, Romania, 18.999
3. Tamara Manina, Soviet Union, 18.733

Floor Exercises
1. Larissa Latynina, Soviet Union, 19.332
2. Elena Teodorescu, Romania, 19.226
3. Eva Bosakova, Czechoslovakia, 19.199

Asymmetric Bars
1. Larissa Latynina, Soviet Union, 19.466
2. Elena Teodorescu, Romania, 19.232
3. Eva Bosakova, Czechoslovakia, 19.066

1958 World Championships, Moscow, Soviet Union

Men

Combined Exercises
1. Boris Shaklin, Soviet Union, 116.05
2. Takashi Ono, Soviet Union, 115.60
3. Yuri Titov, Soviet Union, 115.45
4. Masao Takemoto, Japan, 115.30
5. Pavel Stolbov, Soviet Union, 114.75
Other placings:
28. John Beckner, US, 108.55
33. Nik Stuart, Britain, 108.00
46. Donald Tonri, US, 106.95
53. Abie Grossfeld, US 106.40
54. Larry Banner, US, 106.10
59. Armando Vega, US, 105.75
69. Dick Gradley, Britain, 104.85

Floor Exercises
1. Masao Takemoto, Japan, 19.550
2. Takashi Ono, Japan, 19.500
3. Yuri Titov, Soviet Union, 19.400
4. Nobuyuki Aihara, Japan, 19.350
5. Pavel Stolbov, Soviet Union, 19.175

High Bar
1. Boris Shaklin, Soviet Union, 19.575
2. Albert Azarian, Soviet Union, 19.350
3. equal: Yuri Titov, Soviet Union,
    19.300
    Masao Takemoto, Japan, 19.300
5. Pavel Stolbov, Soviet Union, 19.200

Parallel Bars
1. Boris Shaklin, Soviet Union, 19.650
2. Takashi Ono, Japan, 19.500
3. Pavel Stolbov, Soviet Union, 19.425
4. Yuri Titov, Soviet Union, 19.425
5. Masao Takemoto, Japan, 19.200

Pommel Horse
1. Boris Shaklin, Soviet Union, 19.550
2. Pavel Stolbov, Soviet Union, 19.375
3. Miroslav Cerar, Yugoslavia, 19.350
4. Akira Kono, Japan, 19.125
5. Valentin Lipatov, Soviet Union, 19.075

Vault
1. Yuri Titov, Soviet Union, 19.350
2. Masao Takemoto, Japan, 19.150
3. Takashi Ono, Japan, 19.125
4. Nobuyuki Aihara, Japan, 19.075
5. Yuri Lipatov, Soviet Union, 19.050

Rings
1. Albert Azarian, Soviet Union, 19.875
2. Nobuyuki Aihara, Japan, 19.475
3. Yuri Titov, Soviet Union, 19.455
4. Shinsaku Tsukawaki, Japan, 19.350
5. Masao Takemoto, Japan, 19.300

Women

Combined Exercises
1. Larissa Latynina, Soviet Union, 77.464
2. Eva Bosakova, Czechoslovakia, 76.322
3. Tamara Manina, Soviet Union, 76.167
4. Sofia Mouratova, Soviet Union, 75.897
5. Keiko Tanaka, Japan, 75.797

Team Event
1. Soviet Union, 381.620
2. Czechoslovakia, 371.855
3. Romania, 367.020
4. Japan, 366.951
5. Hungary, 365.387
6. Bulgaria, 365.053
7. China, 363.423
8. Poland, 363.183

Vault
1. Larissa Latynina, Soviet Union, 19.233
2. equal: Sofia Mouratova, Soviet Union, 19.100
   Lidia Kalinina, Soviet Union, 19.100
   Tamara Manina, Soviet Union, 19.100
5. Ann-Sofia Colling, Sweden, 18.832

Beam
1. Larissa Latynina, Soviet Union, 19.399
2. Sofia Mouratova, Soviet Union, 19.099
3. Keiko Tanaka, Japan, 19.066
4. Tamara Manina, Soviet Union, 18.999
5. Eva Bosakova, Czechoslovakia, 18.933

Floor Exercises
1. Eva Bosakova, Czechoslovakia, 19.400
2. Larissa Latynina, Soviet Union, 19.333
3. Keiko Tanaka, Japan, 19.199
4. Sofia Mouratova, Soviet Union, 19.166
5. Tamara Manina, Soviet Union, 19.032

Asymmetric Bars
1. Larissa Latynina, Soviet Union, 19.499
2. Eva Bosakova, Czechoslovakia, 19.300
3. Polina Astakhova, Soviet Union, 19.199
4. Raissa Borissova, Soviet Union, 19.133
5. Tamara Manina, Soviet Union, 19.066

1959 European Championships
Copenhagen, Denmark

Men

Combined Exercises
1. Yuri Titov, Soviet Union, 57.85
2. Pavel Stolbov, Soviet Union, 56.30
3. Phillip Furst, West Germany, 55.45

Floor Exercises
1. Ernst Fivian, Switzerland, 19.20
2. William Thoresson, Sweden, 19.15
3. Yuri Titov, Soviet Union, 18.90

High Bar
1. Pavel Stolbov, Soviet Union, 19.55
2. Yuri Titov, Soviet Union, 19.35
3. equal: Jean Cronstedt, Sweden, 19.05
          Otto Kestola, Finland, 19.05

Parallel Bars
1. Yuri Titov, Soviet Union, 19.15
2. Ferdinand Danis, Czechoslovakia, 18.90
3. Pavel Stolbov, Soviet Union, 18.80

Pommel Horse
1. Yuri Titov, Soviet Union, 19.25
2. Eugen Eckmann, Finland, 18.85
3. Phillip Furst, West Germany, 18.80

Vault
1. equal: William Thoresson, Sweden, 19.30
          Yuri Titov, Soviet Union, 19.30
3. Ernst Fivian, Switzerland, 19.10

Rings
1. Yuri Titov, Soviet Union, 19.60
2. Pavel Stolbov, Soviet Union, 19.50
3. equal: Velik Kapsazov, Bulgaria, 19.25
      Otto Kestola, Finland, 19.25

Cracow, Poland

Women

Combined Exercises
1. Natalie Kot, Poland, 37.833
2. Elena Teodorescu, Romania, 37.767
3. Sonia Iovan, Romania, 37.401

Vault
1. Natalie Kot, Poland, 19.010
2. Vera Caslavska, Czechoslovakia, 18.967
3. Ingrid Fost, East Germany, 18.934

Beam
1. Vera Caslavska, Czechoslovakia, 19.166
2. Sonia Iovan, Romania, 18.867
3. Natalie Kot, Poland, 18.800

Floor Exercises
1. Polina Astakhova, Soviet Union, 19.40
2. Tamara Manina, Soviet Union, 19.20
3. Eva Bosakova, Czechoslovakia, 19.10

Asymmetric Bars
1. Polina Astakhova, Soviet Union, 19.467
2. Elena Teodorescu, 19.200
3. Ingrid Fost, East Germany, 19.034

1960 Olympics, Rome, Italy

Men

Combined Exercises
1. Boris Shaklin, Soviet Union, 115.95
2. Takashi Ono, Japan, 115.90
3. Yuri Titov, Soviet Union, 115.60
4. Shuji Tsurumi, Japan, 114.55
5. equal: Yukio Endo, Japan, 114.45
      Masao Takemoto, Japan, 114.45
Other placings:
21. Larry Banner, US, 111.05
25. Gilbert Backner, US, 110.85
27. Donald Tonry, US, 110.75
36. Abie Grossfeld, US, 110.05
44. Fred Orlofski, US, 109.45
53. Deloid D'Quinn, US, 109.00
55. Nik Stuart, Britain, 108.80
99. Richard Gradley, Britain, 101.75

Team Event
1. Japan, 575.20
2. Soviet Union, 572.70
3. Italy, 559.05
4. Czechoslovakia, 557.15
5. United States, 555.20
6. Finland, 554.45
7. Germany, 553.35
8. Switzerland, 553.35

Other placings:
19. Britain, 510.90

Floor Exercises
1. Nobuyuki Aihara, Japan, 19.450
2. Yuri Titov, Soviet Union, 19.325
3. Franco Menichelli, Italy, 19.275
4. equal: Takashi Mitsukuri, Japan, 19.200
      Takashi Ono, Japan, 19.200

Pommel Horse
1. equal: Eugen Ekmann, Finland, 19.375
      Boris Shaklin, Soviet Union, 19.375
3. Shuji Tsurumi, Japan, 19.150
4. Takashi Mitsukuri, Japan, 19.125
5. Yuri Titov, Soviet Union, 18.950

Vault
1. equal: Boris Shaklin, Soviet Union, 19.350
      Takashi Ono, Japan, 19.350
3. Vladimir Portnoi, Soviet Union, 19.225
4. Yuri Titov, Soviet Union, 19.200
5. Yukio Endo, Japan, 19.175

Rings
1. Albert Azarian, Soviet Union, 19.725
2. Boris Shaklin, Soviet Union, 19.500
3. equal: Takashi Ono, Japan, 19.425
      Velik Kapsasov, Bulgaria, 19.425
5. Nobuyuki Aihara, Japan, 19.400

High Bar
1. Takashi Ono, Japan, 19.600
2. Masao Takemoto, Japan, 19.525
3. Boris Shaklin, Soviet Union, 19.475
4. Yukio Endo, Japan, 19.425
5. equal: Yuri Titov, Soviet Union, 19.400
      Miroslav Cerar, Yugoslavia, 19.400

Parallel Bars
1. Boris Shaklin, Soviet Union, 19.400
2. Giovanni Carminucci, Italy, 19.375
3. Takashi Ono, Japan, 19.350
4. Nobuyuki Aihara, Japan, 19.275
5. Yuri Titov, Soviet Union, 19.200

Women

Combined Exercises
1. Larissa Latynina, Soviet Union, 77.031
2. Sofia Mouratova, Soviet Union, 76.696
3. Polina Astakhova, Soviet Union, 76.164
4. Margit Nikolaeva, Soviet Union, 75.831
5. Sonia Iovan, Romania, 75.797
Other placings :
28. Gail Sontegrath, US, 73.097
39. Doris Fuchs, US, 72.498
44. Sharon Richardson, US, 72.131
51. Betty Maycock, US, 71.930
58. Teresa Montefusco, US, 71.363
70. Muriel Grossfeld, US, 70.132

Team Event
1. Soviet Union, 382.320
2. Czechoslovakia, 373.323
3. Romania, 372.053
4. Japan, 371.422
5. Poland, 368.620
6. Germany, 367.754
7. Hungary, 367.054
8. Bulgaria, 364.920
Other placings :
9. United States, 363.053
17. Britain, 297.721

Vault
1. Margarita Nicolaeva, Soviet Union, 19.316
2. Sofia Mouratova, Soviet Union, 19.049
3. Larissa Latynina, Soviet Union, 19.016
4. Adolfina Tacova, Czechoslovakia, 18.783
5. Sonia Iovan, Romania, 18.766

Beam
1. Eva Bosakova, Czechoslovakia, 19.283
2. Larissa Latynina, Soviet Union, 19.233
3. Sofia Mouratova, Soviet Union, 19.232
4. Margarita Nikolaeva, Soviet Union, 19.183
5. Keiko Ikeda, Japan, 19.132

Floor Exercises
1. Larissa Latynina, Soviet Union, 19.583
2. Polina Astakhova, Soviet Union, 19.532
3. Tamara Ljukina, Soviet Union, 19.449
4. Eva Bosakova, Czechoslovakia, 19.383
5. Sofia Mouratova, Soviet Union, 19.349

Asymmetric Bars
1. Polina Astakhova, Soviet Union, 19.616
2. Larissa Latynina, Soviet Union, 19.416
3. Tamara Ljukina, Soviet Union, 19.399

4. Sofia Mouratova, Soviet Union, 19.382
5. Keiko Ikeda, Japan, 19.333

1961 European Championships

Luxembourg
Men

Combined Exercises
1. Miroslav Cerar, Yugoslavia, 58.05
2. Yuri Titov, Soviet Union, 56.85
3. Giovanni Carminucci, Italy, 56.65

Floor Exercises
1. Franco Menichelli, Italy, 19.45
2. Victor Leontiev, Soviet Union, 19.35
3. Miroslav Cerar, Yugoslavia, 19.30

High Bar
1. Yuri Titov, Soviet Union, 19.50
2. Raymond Csanyi, Hungary, 19.45
3. Otto Kestola, Finland, 19.35

Parallel Bars
1. Miroslav Cerar, Yugoslavia, 19.55
2. Victor Leontiev, Soviet Union, 19.00
3. equal: Giovanni Carminucci, Italy, 18.95
           Franco Menichelli, Italy, 18.95

Pommel Horse
1. Miroslav Cerar, Yugoslavia, 19.60
2. equal: Philip Furst, West Germany, 18.65
           Viktor Leontiev, Soviet Union,
           18.65
Vault
1. Giovanni Carminucci, Italy, 19.35
2. Franco Menichelli, Italy, 19.25
3. equal: Miroslav Cerar, Yugoslavia, 19.20
           Ernst Fivian, Switzerland, 19.20
           William Thoresson, Sweden, 19.20
Rings
1. equal: Miroslav Cerar, Yugoslavia, 19.25
           Viktor Kapsazov, Bulgaria, 19.25
           Yuri Titov, Soviet Union, 19.25

Leipzig, East Germany
Women

Combined Exercises
1. Larissa Latynina, Soviet Union, 38.50
2. Polina Astakhova, Soviet Union, 38.20
3. equal: Ingrid Fost, East Germany, 38.15
           Vera Caslavska, Czechoslovakia,
           38.15

Vault
1. Ute Starke, East Germany, 19.350
2. Ingrid Fost, East Germany, 19.083
3. Natalie Kot, Poland, 19.050

Beam
1. Polina Astakhova, Soviet Union, 19.433
2. Larissa Latynina, Soviet Union, 19.317
3. Ingrid Fost, East Germany, 19.183

Floor Exercises
1. Larissa Latynina, Soviet Union, 19.400
2. Polina Astakhova, Soviet Union, 19.267
3. Vera Caslavska, Czechoslovakia, 19.217

Asymmetric Bars
1. Polina Astakhova, Soviet Union, 19.40
2. Larissa Latynina, Soviet Union, 19.25
3. Ingrid Fost, East Germany, 19.10

1962 World Championships, Prague, Czechoslovakia

Men

Combined Exercises

1. Yuri Titov, Soviet Union, 115.65
2. Yukio Endo, Japan, 115.50
3. Boris Shaklin, Soviet Union, 115.20
4. Takashi Ono, Japan, 115.15
5. Miroslav Cerar, Yugoslavia, 114.95
Other placings:
21. Donald Tonry, US, 111.70
29. Robert Lynn, US, 111.05
35. Armando Vega, US, 110.80
41. Larry Banner, US, 110.50
59. Fred Orlofsky, US, 109.55
73. Nik Stuart, Britain, 108.70
85. Abie Grossfeld, US, 108.00
96. Dick Gradley, Britain, 106.50

Team Event
1. Japan, 574.65
2. Soviet Union, 573.15
3. Czechoslovakia, 561.50
4. China, 559.00
5. Italy, 557.20
6. United States, 555.20
7. Finland, 554.90
8. East Germany, 554.50

Floor Exercises
1. equal: Nobuyuki Aihara, Japan, 19.500
              Yukio Endo, Japan, 19.500
3. Franco Menichelli, Italy, 19.450
4. Haruhiro Yamashita, Japan, 19.300

High Bar
1. Takashi Ono, Japan, 19.675
2. equal: Yukio Endo, Japan, 19.625
              Pavel Stolbov, Soviet Union, 19.625
4. equal: Yuri Titov, Soviet Union, 19.500
              Takashi Mitsukuri, Japan, 19.500
5. Takashi Ono, Japan, 19.275

Parallel Bars
1. Miroslav Cerar, Yugoslavia, 19.625
2. Boris Shaklin, Soviet Union, 19.600
3. Yukio Endo, Japan, 19.500
4. Haruhiro Yamashita, Japan, 19.375
5. Takashi Ono, Japan, 19.250

Pommel Horse
1. Miroslav Cerar, Yugoslavia, 19.750
2. Boris Shaklin, Soviet Union, 19.375
3. equal: Takashi Mitsukuri, Japan, 19.300
              Yu Lieh-feng, China, 19.300
5. Yuri Titov, Soviet Union, 19.275

Vault
1. Premysel Krbec, Czechoslovakia, 19.550
2. Haruhiro Yamashita, Japan, 19.350
3. equal: Boris Shaklin, Soviet Union, 19.225
              Yukio Endo, Japan, 19.225
5. Takashi Ono, Japan, 19.175

Rings
1. Yuri Titov, Soviet Union, 19.550
2. equal: Yukio Endo, Japan, 19.425
              Boris Shaklin, Soviet Union, 19.425
4. Nobuyuki Aihara, Japan, 19.250
5. Viktor Leontiev, Soviet Union, 19.225

Women
Combined Exercises
1. Larissa Latynina, Soviet Union, 78.030
2. Vera Caslavska, Czechoslovakia, 77.732
3. Irina Pervuschina, Soviet Union, 77.465
4. Eva Bosakova, Czechoslovakia, 76.898
5. Tamara Manina, Soviet Union, 76.865
Other placings:
31. Muriel Grossfeld, US, 74.331
40. Doris Fuchs, US, 73.897
50. Betty Maycock, US, 73.231

54. Marie McNalther, US, 73.096
59. Avis Tibber, US, 72.730
63. Gail Sontegrath, US, 72.165
89. Monica Rutherford, Britain, 69.597
96. Denise Goddard, Britain, 67.762

Vault
1. Vera Caslavska, Czechoslovakia, 19.649
2. Larissa Latynina, Soviet Union, 19.632
3. Tamara Manina, Soviet Union, 19.549
4. Brigit Radochla, East Germany, 19.483
5. Ingrid Fost, East Germany, 19.466

Beam
1. Eva Bosakova, Czechoslovakia, 19.499
2. Larissa Latynina, Soviet Union, 19.416
3. equal: Keiko Ikeda, Japan, 19.366
        Aniko Ducza, Hungary, 19.366
5. Vera Caslavska, Czechoslovakia, 19.333

Floor Exercises
1. Larissa Latynina, Soviet Union, 19.716
2. Irina Pervuschina, Soviet Union, 19.616
3. Vera Caslavska, Czechoslovakia, 19.550
4. equal: Polina Astakhova, Soviet Union, 19.446
        Eva Bosakova, Czechoslovakia, 19.446

Asymmetric Bars
1. Irina Pervuschina, Soviet Union, 19.566
2. Eva Bosakova, Czechoslovakia, 19.466
3. Larissa Latynina, Soviet Union, 19.499
4. Polina Astakhova, Soviet Union, 19.399
5. Vera Caslavska, Czechoslovakia, 19.366

1963 European Championships

Belgrade, Yugoslavia

Men

Combined Exercises
1. Miroslav Cerar, Yugoslavia, 57.75
2. Boris Shaklin, Soviet Union, 57.65
3. Vladimir Kerdemelidi, Soviet Union, 57.45

Floor Exercises
1. Franco Menichelli, Italy, 19.55
2. Vladimir Kerdemelidi, Soviet Union, 19.45
3. Miroslav Cerar, Yugoslavia, 19.15

High Bar
1. equal: Miroslav Cerar, Yugoslavia, 19.70
        Boris Shaklin, Soviet Union, 19.70
3. Vladimir Kerdemelidi, Soviet Union, 19.50

Parallel Bars
1. Giovanni Carminucci, Italy, 19.40
2. Boris Shaklin, Soviet Union, 19.25
3. Franco Menichelli, Italy, 19.20

Pommel Horse
1. Miroslav Cerar, Yugoslavia, 19.65
2. Vladimir Kerdemelidi, Soviet Union, 19.40
3. Boris Shaklin, Soviet Union, 19.35

Vault
1. Premysil Krbec, Czechoslovakia, 19.55
2. Miroslav Cerar, Yugoslavia, 19.05
3. equal: Vladimir Kerdemelidi, Soviet Union, 18.95
        Martin Srot, Yugoslavia, 18.95

Rings
1. equal: Miroslav Cerar, Yugoslavia, 19.25
        Velik Kapsazov, Bulgaria, 19.25
        Boris Shaklin, Soviet Union, 19.25

Paris, France

Women

Combined Exercises
1. Mirjana Bilic, Yugoslavia, 37.232
2. Solveig Egman, Sweden, 37.131
3. Eva Rydell, Sweden, 36.966

Vault
1. Solveig Egman, Sweden, 19.032
2. Thea Belmer, Holland, 18.799
3. Jannie Viersta, Holland, 18.732

Beam
1. Eva Rydell, Sweden, 19.033
2. Kosanyi Kocis, Yugoslavia, 18.500
3. Solveig Bilic, Yugoslavia, 18.400

Floor Exercises
1. Mirjana Bilic, Yugoslavia, 18.932
2. Solveig Egman, Sweden, 18.899
3. Kosanyi Kocis, Yugoslavia, 18.766

Asymmetric Bars
1. Thea Belmer, Holland, 18.766
2. Kosanyi Kocis, Yugoslavia, 18.733
3. Solveig Egman, Sweden, 18.566

1964 Olympics, Tokyo, Japan

Men

Combined Exercises
1. Yukio Endo, Japan, 115.95
2. equal: Boris Shaklin, Soviet Union, 115.40
        Shuji Tsurumi, Soviet Union, 115.40
        Viktor Lisitsky, Soviet Union, 115.40
5. Franco Menichelli, Italy, 115.15
Other placings:
20. Makoto Sakamoto, US, 112.40
32. Russell Mitchell, US, 111.20
39. Ronald Barak, US, 110.95
55. Larry Banner, US, 110.05
58. Gregor Weiss, US, 109.90
68. Arthur Shurlock, US, 109.10

Team Event
1. Japan, 577.95
2. Soviet Union, 575.45
3. Germany, 565.10
4. Italy, 560.90
5. Poland, 559.50
6. Czechoslovakia, 558.15
7. United States, 556.95
8. Finland, 556.20

Floor Exercises
1. Franco Menichelli, Italy, 19.45
2. equal: Viktor Lisitsky, Soviet Union, 19.35
        Yukio Endo, Japan, 19.35
4. Viktor Leontiev, Soviet Union, 19.20
5. Takashi Mitsukuri, Japan, 19.10

High Bar
1. Boris Shaklin, Soviet Union, 19.625
2. Yuri Titov, Soviet Union, 19.550
3. Miroslav Cerar, Yugoslavia, 19.500
4. Viktor Lisitsky, Soviet Union, 19.325
5. Yukio Endo, Japan, 19.050

Parallel Bars
1. Yukio Endo, Japan, 19.675
2. Shuji Tsurumi, Japan, 19.450
3. Franco Menichelli, Italy, 19.350
4. Sergei Diamidov, Soviet Union, 19.225
5. Viktor Lisitsky, Soviet Union, 19.200

Pommel Horse
1. Miroslav Cerar, Yugoslavia, 19.525
2. Shuji Tsumuri, Japan, 19.325

3. Yuri Tsapenko, Soviet Union, 19.200
4. Haruhiro Yamashita, Japan, 19.075
5. Herald Wigaard, Norway, 18.925

Vault
1. Haruhiro Yamashita, Japan, 19.600
2. Viktor Lisitsky, Soviet Union, 19.325
3. Hannu Rantakari, Finland, 19.300
4. Shuji Tsurumi, Soviet Union, 19.225
5. Boris Shaklin, Soviet Union, 19.200

Rings
1. Takuji Hayata, Japan, 19.475
2. Franco Menichelli, Italy, 19.425
3. Boris Shaklin, Soviet Union, 19.400
4. Viktor Leontiev, Soviet Union, 19.350
5. Shuji Tsurumi, Japan, 19.275

Women

Combined Exercises
1. Vera Caslavska, Czechoslovakia, 77.564
2. Larissa Latynina, Soviet Union, 76.998
3. Polina Astakhova, Soviet Union, 76.965
4. Brigit Radochla, Germany, 76.431
5. Hana Ruzickova, Czechoslovakia, 76.097
Other placings:
34. D. E. McClements, US, 74.064
36. Linda Jo Metheney, US, 73.998
51. Kathleen Corrigan, US, 72.831
58. Muriel Grossfeld, US, 72.064
60. Marie Sue Walther, US, 72.031
62. Janie Lee Speaks, US, 71.864
71. Denise Goddard, Britain, 69.365
77. Monica Rutherford, Britain, 68.065

Team Event
1. Soviet Union, 380.890
2. Czechoslovakia, 379.989
3. Japan, 377.889
4. Germany, 376.038
5. Hungary, 375.445
6. Romania, 371.984
7. Poland, 371.287
8. Sweden, 367.888
9. United States, 367.321

Vault
1. Vera Caslavska, Czechoslovakia, 19.483
2. equal: Larissa Latynina, Soviet Union, 19.283
        Brigit Radochla, Germany, 19.283
4. Toshiko Aihara, Japan, 19.282
5. Elena Volchetskaya, Soviet Union, 19.149

Beam
1. Vera Caslavska, Czechoslovakia, 19.449
2. Tamara Manina, Soviet Union, 19.399
3. Larissa Latynina, Soviet Union, 19.382
4. Polina Astakhova, Soviet Union, 19.366
5. Hana Ruzickova, Czechoslovakia, 19.349

Floor Exercises
1. Larissa Latynina, Soviet Union, 19.599
2. Polina Astakhova, Soviet Union, 19.500
3. Ducza Janosi, Hungary, 19.300
4. Brigit Radochla, Germany, 19.299
5. Ingrid Fost, Germany, 19.266

Asymmetric Bars
1. Polina Astakhova, Soviet Union, 19.332
2. Katalin Makray, Hungary, 19.216
3. Larissa Latynina, Soviet Union, 19.199
4. Toshiko Aihara, Japan, 18.782
5. Vera Caslavska, Czechoslovakia, 18.416

1965 European Championships

Antwerp, Belgium

Men

Combined Exercises
1. Franco Menichelli, Italy, 57.55
2. Viktor Lisitsky, Soviet Union, 57.50
3. Sergei Diamidov, Soviet Union, 56.95

Floor Exercises
1. Franco Menichelli, Italy, 19.50
2. equal: Miroslav Cerar, Yugoslavia, 18.95
        Viktor Lisitsky, Soviet Union,
        18.95

High Bar
1. Franco Menichelli, Italy, 19.55
2. Viktor Lisitsky, Soviet Union, 19.40
3. Sergei Diamidov, Soviet Union, 19.35

Parallel Bars
1. Miroslav Cerar, Yugoslavia, 19.50
2. Franco Menichelli, Italy, 19.35
3. equal: Sergei Diamidov, Soviet Union,
        19.25
        Erwin Koppe, East Germany, 19.25

Pommel Horse
1. Viktor Lisitsky, Soviet Union, 19.39
2. Miroslav Cerar, Yugoslavia, 19.25
3. equal: Sergei Diamidov, Soviet Union,
        19.20
        Olli Laiho, Finland, 19.20

Vault
1. Viktor Lisitsky, Soviet Union, 19.10
2. equal: Gueorgui Adamov, Bulgaria, 18.95
        Raimo Heinonen, Finland, 18.95
        Age Storhaug, Norway, 18.95

Rings
1. equal: Viktor Lisitsky, Soviet Union, 19.35
        Franco Menichelli, Italy, 19.35
3. Miroslav Cerar, Yugoslavia, 19.25

Sofia, Bulgaria

Women

Combined Exercises
1. Vera Caslavska, Czechoslovakia, 38.899
2. Larissa Latynina, Soviet Union, 38.198
3. Brigit Radochla, East Germany, 37.998

Vault
1. Vera Caslavska, Czechoslovakia, 19.750
2. Ute Starke, East Germany, 19.500
3. Larissa Latynina, Soviet Union, 19.366

Beam
1. Vera Caslavska, Czechoslovakia, 19.433
2. Larissa Latynina, Soviet Union, 19.229
3. equal: Larissa Petrik, Soviet Union,
        19.099
        Brigit Radochla, East Germany,
        19.099

Floor Exercises
1. Vera Caslavska, Czechoslovakia, 19.333
2. equal: Larissa Latynina, Soviet Union,
        19.066
        Brigit Radochla, East Germany,
        19.066

Asymmetric Bars
1. Vera Caslavska, Czechoslovakia, 19.633
2. Larissa Latynina, Soviet Union, 19.329
3. Maria Karaschka, Bulgaria, 19.299

1966 World Championships, Dortmund, West Germany

Men

Combined Exercises
1. Mikhail Voronin, Soviet Union, 116.15
2. Shuji Tsurumi, Japan, 115.25
3. Akinori Nakayama, Japan, 114.95
4. Miroslav Cerar, Yugoslavia, 114.75
5. Franco Menichelli, Italy, 114.65

Other placings:
16. Mokoto Sakamoto, US, 112.15
34. Greg Weiss, US, 109.75
35. Fred Roethlisberger, US, 109.55
39. Steve Cohen, US, 109.25
49. Arno Lascari, US, 108.25
58. Donald Tonry, US, 106.80
84. John Pancott, Britain, 102.75
92. Dick Gradley, Britain, 102.35
94. Robert Williams, Britain, 102.05

Team Event
1. Japan, 575.15
2. Soviet Union, 570.90
3. East Germany, 561.00
4. Czechoslovakia, 551.20
5. Poland, 550.60
6. United States, 550.40
7. Yugoslavia, 548.15
8. West Germany, 548.00
Other placings:
17. Britain, 509.05

Floor Exercises
1. Akinori Nakayama, Japan, 19.400
2. Yukio Endo, Japan, 19.375
3. Franco Menichelli, Italy, 19.300
4. Takeshi Kato, Japan, 19.225
5. Valeri Karassev, Soviet Union, 19.000

High Bar
1. Akinori Nakayama, Japan, 19.675
2. Yukio Endo, Japan, 19.600
3. Takeshi Mitsukuri, Japan, 19.425
4. equal: Miroslav Cerar, Yugoslavia,
        19.400
        Mikhail Voronin, Soviet Union,
        19.400

Parallel Bars
1. Sergei Diamidov, Soviet Union, 19.550
2. Mikhail Voronin, Soviet Union, 19.400
3. Miroslav Cerar, Yugoslavia, 19.350
4. Franco Menichelli, Italy, 19.225
5. Mathias Brehme, East Germany, 19.200

Pommel Horse
1. Miroslav Cerar, Yugoslavia, 19.525
2. Mikhail Voronin, Soviet Union, 19.325
3. Takeshi Kato, Japan, 19.125
4. Mathias Brehme, East Germany,
        19.025
5. Shuji Tsurumi, Japan, 19.000

Vault
1. Haruhiro Matsuda, Japan, 19.425
2. Takeshi Kato, Japan, 19.325
3. Akinori Nakayama, Japan, 19.050
4. Yukio Endo, Japan, 18.700
5. Mikhail Voronin, Soviet Union, 18.650

Rings
1. Mikhail Voronin, Soviet Union, 19.750
2. Akinori Nakayama, Japan, 19.500
3. Franco Menichelli, Italy, 19.475
4. Takeshi Kato, Japan, 19.300
5. Sergei Diamidov, Soviet Union, 19.200

Women

Combined Exercises
1. Vera Caslavska, Czechoslovakia,
        78.298
2. Natalia Kuchinskaya, Soviet Union,
        78.087
3. Keiko Ikeda, Japan, 76.997
4. Erika Zuchold, East Germany, 76.596
5. Jaroslava Sedlackova, Czechoslovakia,
        76.465
Other placings:
27. Doris Brause, US, 74.297
33. Kathy Gleason, US, 73.864
40. Joce Tanac, US, 72.964
48. Caroline Hacker, US, 72.397
50. Debbie Bailey, US, 72.197
81. Mary Prestidge, Britain, 69.932
90. Margaret Bell, Britain, 69.096

Vault
1. Vera Caslavska, Czechoslovakia,
        19.583
2. Erika Zuchold, East Germany, 19.399
3. Natalia Kuchinskaya, Soviet Union,
        19.316
4. Ute Starke, East Germany, 19.216
5. Jana Krajcirova, Czechoslovakia,
        19.199

Beam
1. Natalia Kuchinskaya, Soviet Union,
        19.650
2. Vera Caslavska, Czechoslovakia,
        19.333
3. Larissa Petrik, Soviet Union, 19.250
4. Keiko Ikeda, Japan, 19.233
5. Janosi Ducza, Hungary, 19.233

Floor Exercises
1. Natalia Kuchinskaya, Soviet Union, 19.733
2. Vera Caslavska, Czechoslovakia, 19.683
3. Zinaida Drouginina, Soviet Union, 19.666
4. Larissa Petrik, Soviet Union, 19.416
5. Jana Kubickova, Czechoslovakia, 19.363

Asymmetric Bars
1. Natalia Kuchinskaya, Soviet Union, 19.616
2. Keiko Ikeda, Japan, 19.566
3. Taniko Mitsukuri, Japan, 19.516
4. Vera Caslavska, Czechoslovakia, 19.482
5. Polina Astakhova, Soviet Union, 19.146

1967 European Championships

Tampere, Finland

Men

Combined Exercises
1. Mikhail Voronin, Soviet Union, 58.00
2. Viktor Lisitsky, Soviet Union, 57.30
3. Franco Menichelli, Italy, 57.25

Floor Exercises
1. Lasse Laine, Finland, 19.15
2. Franco Menichelli, Italy, 19.10
3. Nicolai Kubica, Poland, 18.80

High Bar
1. Viktor Lisitsky, Soviet Union, 19.45
2. Mikhail Voronin, Soviet Union, 19.40
3. equal: Miroslav Cerar, Yugoslavia, 19.15
   Franco Menichelli, Italy, 19.15

Parallel Bars
1. Mikhail Voronin, Soviet Union, 19.40
2. Franco Menichelli, Italy, 19.30
3. Giovanni Carminucci, Italy, 19.20

Pommel Horse
1. Mikhail Voronin, Soviet Union, 19.55
2. Miroslav Cerar, Yugoslavia, 19.20
3. Gerhard Dietrich, East Germany, 18.90

Vault
1. Viktor Lisitsky, Soviet Union, 19.200
2. Gueorgui Adamov, Bulgaria, 18.775
3. Gerhard Dietrich, East Germany, 18.175

Rings
1. equal: Viktor Lisitsky, Soviet Union, 19.40
   Mikhail Voronin, Soviet Union, 19.40
3. Nicolai Kubica, Poland, 19.10

Amsterdam, Holland

Women

Combined Exercises
1. Vera Caslavska, Czechoslovakia, 38.965
2. Zinaida Drouginina, Soviet Union, 38.553
3. Maria Kraycirovaj, Czechoslovakia, 38.199

Vault
1. Vera Caslavska, Czechoslovakia, 19.733
2. Erika Zuchold, East Germany, 19.553
3. Karin Janz, East Germany, 19.333

Beam
1. Vera Caslavska, Czechoslovakia, 19.883
2. Natalia Kuchinskaya, Soviet Union, 19.666
3. Zinaida Drouginina, Soviet Union, 19.499

Floor Exercises
1. Vera Caslavska, Czechoslovakia, 19.886
2. Natalia Kuchinskaya, Soviet Union, 19.733
3. Zinaida Drouginina, Soviet Union, 19.666

Asymmetric Bars
1. Vera Caslavska, Czechoslovakia, 19.199
2. Karin Janz, East Germany, 19.166
3. Maria Kraycirovaj, Czechoslovakia, 19.066

1968 Olympics, Mexico City, Mexico

Men

Combined Exercises
1. Sawao Kato, Japan, 115.90
2. Mikhail Voronin, Soviet Union, 115.85
3. Akinori Nakayama, Japan, 115.65
4. Eizo Kenmotsu, Japan, 114.90
5. Takeshi Kato, Japan, 114.85
Other placings :
34. Fred Roethlisberger, US, 109.70
36. Steve Hug, US, 109.60
46. Steve Cohen, US, 108.75
57. Sidney Freudenstein, US, 108.00
79. Stan Wild, Britain, 105.50

80. Kanati Allen, US, 105.45
91. Michael Booth, Britain, 103.65

Team Event
1. Japan, 575.90
2. Soviet Union, 571.10
3. East Germany, 557.15
4. Czechoslovakia, 557.10
5. Poland, 555.40
6. Yugoslavia, 550.75
7. United States, 548.90
8. West Germany, 548.35

Floor Exercises
1. Sawao Kato, Japan, 19.475
2. Akinori Nakayama, Japan, 19.400
3. Takashi Kato, Japan, 19.275
4. Mitsuo Tsukahara, Japan, 19.050
5. Valeri Karassev, Soviet Union, 18.950

High Bar
1. equal: Mikhail Voronin, Soviet Union, 19.550
        Akinori Nakayama, Japan, 19.550
3. Eizo Kenmotsu, Japan, 19.375
4. Klaus Koste, East Germany, 19.225
5. Sergei Diamidov, Soviet Union, 19.150

Parallel Bars
1. Akinori Nakayama, Japan, 19.475
2. Mikhail Voronin, Soviet Union, 19.425
3. Vladimir Klimenko, Soviet Union, 19.225
4. Takeshi Kato, Japan, 19.200
5. Eizo Kenmotsu, Japan, 19.175

Pommel Horse
1. Miroslav Cerar, Yugoslavia, 19.325
2. Olli Laiho, Finland, 19.225
3. Mikhail Voronin, Soviet Union, 19.200
4. Wilhelm Kubica, Poland, 19.150
5. Eizo Kenmotsu, Japan, 19.050

Vault
1. Mikhail Voronin, Soviet Union, 19.000
2. Yukio Endo, Japan, 18.950
3. Sergei Diamidov, Soviet Union, 18.925
4. Takeshi Kato, Japan, 18.775
5. Akinori Nakayama, Japan, 18.725

Rings
1. Akinori Nakayama, Japan, 19.450
2. Mikhail Voronin, Soviet Union, 19.325
3. Sawao Kato, Japan, 19.225
4. Mitsuo Tsukahara, Japan, 19.125
5. Takeshi Kato, Japan, 19.050

Women
Combined Exercises
1. Vera Caslavska, Czechoslovakia, 78.25
2. Zinaida Voronina, Soviet Union, 76.85
3. Natalia Kuchinskaya, Soviet Union, 76.75
4. equal: Larissa Petrik, Soviet Union, 76.70
        Erika Zuchold, East Germany, 76.70
Other placings:
16. Cathy Rigby, US, 74.95
28. Linda Metheny, US, 74.00
30. Joyce Tanac, US, 73.65
31. Kathy Gleason, US, 73.60
34. Coleen Mulvihill, US, 73.05
39. Wendy Cluff, US, 71.80
74. Margaret Bell, Britain, 67.95
88. Mary Prestidge, Britain, 65.60

Team Event
1. Soviet Union, 382.85
2. Czechoslovakia, 382.20
3. East Germany, 379.10
4. Japan, 375.45
5. Hungary, 369.80
6. United States, 369.75
7. France, 361.75
8. Bulgaria, 355.10

Vault
1. Vera Caslavska, Czechoslovakia, 19.775
2. Erika Zuchold, East Germany, 19.625
3. Zinaida Voronina, Soviet Union, 19.500
4. Mariana Krajcirova, Czechoslovakia, 19.475
5. Natalia Kuchinskaya, Soviet Union, 19.375

Beam
1. Natalia Kuchinskaya, Soviet Union, 19.650
2. Vera Caslavska, Czechoslovakia, 19.575
3. Larissa Petrik, Soviet Union, 19.250
4. equal: Karin Janz, East Germany, 19.225
        Linda Metheny, US, 19.225

Floor Exercises
1. equal: Larissa Petrik, Soviet Union, 19.675
        Vera Caslavska, Czechoslovakia, 19.675
3. Natalia Kuchinskaya, Soviet Union, 19.650
4. Zinaida Voronina, Soviet Union, 19.550

5. equal: Bohumila Rimnacova,
        Czechoslovakia, 19.325
        Olga Karaseva, Soviet Union,
        19.325

Asymmetric Bars
1. Vera Caslavska, Czechoslovakia, 19.650
2. Karin Janz, East Germany, 19.500
3. Zinaida Voronina, Soviet Union, 19.425
4. Bohumila Rimnacova, Czechoslovakia,
   19.350
5. Erika Zuchold, East Germany, 19.325

1969 European Championships
Warsaw, Poland

Men

Combined Exercises
1. Mikhail Voronin, Soviet Union, 57.45
2. Viktor Klimenko, Soviet Union, 57.00
3. Mikolai Kubica, Poland, 56.85

Floor Exercises
1. Raytche Christov, Bulgaria, 19.20
2. Viktor Lisitsky, Soviet Union, 18.85
3. Sylwester Kubica, Poland, 18.80

High Bar
1. equal: Viktor Kliménko, Soviet Union,
        19.25
        Viktor Lisitsky, Soviet Union, 19.25
3. Miroslav Cerar, Yugoslavia, 19.20

Parallel Bars
1. Mikhail Voronin, Soviet Union, 19.05
2. equal: Miroslav Cerar, Yugoslavia, 18.95
        Viktor Klimenko, Soviet Union,
        18.95

Pommel Horse
1. equal: Miroslav Cerar, Yugoslavia, 19.50
        Wilhelm Kubica, Poland, 19.50
3. Mikhail Voronin, Soviet Union, 19.45

Vault
1. Viktor Klimenko, Soviet Union, 18.65
2. equal: Nikolai Kubica, Poland, 18.55
        Mikhail Voronin, Soviet Union,
        18.55

Rings
1. Mikhail Voronin, Soviet Union, 19.50
2. equal: Viktor Klimenko, Soviet Union,
        19.30
        Nikolai Kubica, Poland, 19.30

Landskrona, Sweden
Women

Combined Exercises
1. Karin Janz, East Germany, 38.65
2. Olga Karaseva, Soviet Union, 38.10
3. equal: Ludmila Tourischeva, Soviet
        Union, 37.90
        Erika Zuchold, East Germany,
        37.90

Vault
1. Karin Janz, East Germany, 19.70
2. Erika Zuchold, East Germany, 19.45
3. Olga Karaseva, Soviet Union, 19.40

Beam
1. Karin Janz, East Germany, 19.05
2. Olga Karaseva, Soviet Union, 18.95
3. Jindra Kostalova, Czechoslovakia, 18.75

Floor Exercises
1. Olga Karaseva, Soviet Union, 19.45
2. Karin Janz, East Germany, 19.40
3. equal: Jindra Kostalova, Czechoslovakia,
        19.10
        Ludmila Tourischeva, Soviet
        Union, 19.10

Asymmetric Bars
1. Karin Janz, East Germany, 19.65
2. Olga Karaseva, Soviet Union, 19.45
3. Ludmila Tourischeva, Soviet Union, 19.40

1970 World Championships, Ljubljana, Yugoslavia

Men

Combined Exercises
1. Eizo Kenmotsu, Japan, 115.05
2. Mitsuo Tsukahara, Japan, 113.85.
3. Akinori Nakayama, Japan, 113.80
4. Mikhail Voronin, Soviet Union, 113.75
5. Viktor Klimenko, Soviet Union, 113.60
Other placings :
12. Makoto Sakamoto, US, 111.65
33. Kanati Allen, US, 107.65
58. Marshall Avener, US, 105.20
59. Brent Simmons. US, 105.15
60. George Greenfield, US, 105.00
80. Thomas Lindner, US, 102.15
85. Stan Wild, Britain, 101.70
91. Bill Norgrove, Britain, 101.00

Team Event
1. Japan, 571.10
2. Soviet Union, 564.35
3. East Germany, 553.15
4. Yugoslavia, 549.45
5. Poland, 547.05
6. Switzerland, 541.75
7. United States, 537.60
8. Romania, 536.55
Other placings:
17. Britain, 502.80

Floor Exercises
1. Akinori Nakayama, Japan, 19.025
2. Eizo Kenmotsu, Japan, 18.975
3. Takeshi Kato, Japan, 18.900
4. Baytcho Hristov, Bulgaria, 18.875
5. Mitsuo Tsukahara, Japan, 18.800

High Bar
1. Eizo Kenmotsu, Japan, 19.475
2. Akinori Nakayama, Japan, 19.375
3. equal: Takuji Hayata, Japan, 19.350
          Klaus Koste, East Germany, 19.350
5. Mikhail Voronin, Soviet Union, 19.275

Parallel Bars
1. Akinori Nakayama, Japan, 19.400
2. equal: Eizo Kenmotsu, Japan 19.250
          Mikhail Voronin, Soviet Union, 19.250
4. Takeshi Kato, Japan, 19.200
5. Viktor Klimenko, Soviet Union, 19.175

Pommel Horse
1. Miroslav Cerar, Yugoslavia, 19.375
2. Eizo Kenmotsu, Japan, 19.325
3. Viktor Klimenko, Soviet Union, 19.050
4. Milko Vratic, Yugoslavia, 19.000
5. Mathias Brehme, East Germany, 18.875

Vault
1. Mitsuo Tsukahara, Japan, 19.125
2. Viktor Klimenko, Soviet Union, 19.000
3. Takeshi Kato, Japan, 18.600
4. Fumio Honma, Japan, 18.325
5. Eizo Kenmotsu, Japan, 18.125

Rings
1. Akinori Nakayama, Japan, 19.400
2. Mitsuo Tsukahara, Japan, 19.250
3. Mikhail Voronin, Soviet Union, 19.225
4. equal: Eizo Kenmotsu, Japan, 18.900
          Takuji Hayata, Japan, 18.900

Women
Combined Exercises
1. Ludmila Tourischeva, Soviet Union, 77.05
2. Erika Zuchold, East Germany, 76.45
3. Zinaida Voronina, Soviet Union, 76.15
4. Karin Janz, East Germany, 76.00
5. Ljubov Burda, Soviet Union, 75.85
Other placings:
15. Cathy Rigby, US, 74.45
33. equal: Joan Moore, US, 71.80
          Adele Gleaves, US, 71.80
44. Wendy Cliff, US, 71.05
49. Celo Carfer, US, 70.30
61. Kim Chase, US, 69.30

Team Event
1. Soviet Union, 380.65
2. East Germany, 377.75
3. Czechoslovakia, 371.90
4. Japan, 371.75
5. Romania, 364.50
6. Hungary, 362.80
7. United States, 360.20
8. West Germany, 356.85
Other placings:
19. Britain, 325.65

Vault
1. Erika Zuchold, East Germany, 19.450
2. Karin Janz, East Germany, 19.350
3. equal: Ludmila Tourischeva, Soviet Union, 19.300
          Ljubov Burda, Soviet Union, 19.300
5. Marcela Vachova, Czechoslovakia, 19.275

Beam
1. Erika Zuchold, East Germany, 19.200
2. Cathy Rigby, US, 19.050
3. equal: Christine Schmidt, East Germany, 18.900
          Larissa Petrik, Soviet Union, 18.900
5. Angelika Hellmann, East Germany, 18.850

Floor Exercises
1. Ludmila Tourischeva, Soviet Union, 19.650
2. Olga Karaseva, Soviet Union, 19.525
3. Zinaida Voronina, Soviet Union, 19.375
4. Karin Janz, East Germany, 19.200
5. Miyuki Matsuhisa, Japan, 19.075

Asymmetric Bars
1. Karin Janz, East Germany, 19.550
2. Ludmila Tourischeva, Soviet Union, 19.450
3. Zinaida Voronina, Soviet Union, 19.300
4. equal: Marianne Nemethova, Czechoslovakia, 19.275
   Ljubov Burda, Soviet Union, 19.275

1971 European Championships

Madrid, Spain

Men

Combined Exercises
1. Viktor Klimenko, Soviet Union, 56.90
2. Mikhail Voronin, Soviet Union, 56.70
3. Nikolai Andrianov, Soviet Union, 56.25

Floor Exercises
1. Raytche Christov, Bulgaria, 19.10
2. Jose Gines, Spain, 18.75
3. Nikolai Andrianov, Soviet Union, 18.70

High Bar
1. Klaus Koste, East Germany, 19.05
2. Mikhail Voronin, Soviet Union, 18.95
3. Roland Hurzeler, Switzerland, 18.85

Parallel Bars
1. Giovanni Carminucci, Italy, 18.85
2. equal: Nikolai Andrianov, Soviet Union, 18.80
   Klaus Koste, East Germany, 18.80
   Mikhail Voronin, Soviet Union, 18.80

Pommel Horse
1. Nikolai Andrianov, Soviet Union, 18.90
2. Mathias Brehme, East Germany, 18.75
3. Mikhail Voronin, Soviet Union, 18.70

Vault
1. Nikolai Andrianov, Soviet Union, 18.750
2. Andrej Szajna, Poland, 18.675
3. Klaus Koste, East Germany, 18.500

Rings
1. Mikhail Voronin, Soviet Union, 19.25
2. Nikolai Andrianov, Soviet Union, 18.80
3. Andrej Szajna, Poland, 18.70

Minsk, Soviet Union

Women

Combined Exercises
1. equal: Ludmila Tourischeva, Soviet Union, 38.85
   Tamara Lazakovitch, Soviet Union, 38.85
3. Erika Zuchold, East Germany, 38.30

Vault
1. Ludmila Tourischeva, Soviet Union, 19.60
2. Tamara Lazakovitch, Soviet Union, 19.55
3. Erika Zuchold, East Germany, 19.50

Beam
1. Tamara Lazakovitch, Soviet Union, 19.20
2. Ludmila Tourischeva, Soviet Union, 19.15
3. Erika Zuchold, East Germany, 19.00

Floor Exercises
1. Ludmila Tourischeva, Soviet Union, 19.65
2. Tamara Lazakovitch, Soviet Union, 19.60
3. Erika Zuchold, East Germany, 19.25

Asymmetric Bars
1. Tamara Lazakovitch, Soviet Union, 19.35
2. Ludmila Tourischeva, Soviet Union, 19.20
3. Angelika Hellmann, East Germany, 19.00

1972 Olympics, Munich, West Germany

Men

Combined Exercises
1. Sawao Kato, Japan, 114.650
2. Eizo Kenmotsu, Japan, 114.575
3. Akinori Nakayama, Japan, 114.325
4. Nikolai Andrianov, Soviet Union, 114.200
5. Shigeru Kasamatsu, Japan, 113.700
Other placings :
31. Steven Hug, US, 108.875

Team Event
1. Japan, 571.25
2. Soviet Union, 564.05
3. East Germany, 559.70
4. Poland, 551.10
5. West Germany, 546.40
6. North Korea, 545.05
7. Romania, 538.90
8. Hungary, 538.60

Other placings:
10. United States, 533.85

Floor Exercises
1. Nikolai Andrianov, Soviet Union, 19.175
2. Akinori Nakayama, Japan, 19.125
3. Shigeru Kasamatsu, Japan, 19.025
4. Eizo Kenmotsu, Japan, 18.925
5. Klaus Koste, East Germany, 18.825

High Bar
1. Mitsuo Tsukahara, Japan, 19.725
2. Sawao Kato, Japan, 19.525
3. Shigeru Kasamatsu, Japan, 19.450
4. Eizo Kenmotsu, Japan, 19.350
5. Akinori Nakayama, Japan, 19.225

Parallel Bars
1. Sawao Kato, Japan, 19.475
2. Shigeru Kasamatsu, Japan, 19.375
3. Eizo Kenmotsu, Japan, 19.250
4. Viktor Klimenko, Soviet Union, 19.125
5. Akinori Nakayama, Japan, 18.875

Pommel Horse
1. Viktor Klimenko, Soviet Union, 19.125
2. Sawao Kato, Japan, 19.000
3. Eizo Kenmotsu, Japan, 18.950
4. Shigeru Kasamatsu, Japan, 18.925
5. Mikhail Voronin, Soviet Union, 18.875

Vault
1. Klaus Koste, East Germany, 18.850
2. Viktor Klimenko, Soviet Union, 18.825
3. Nikolai Andrianov, Soviet Union, 18.800
4. equal: Eizo Kenmotsu, Japan, 18.550
             Sawao Kato, Japan, 18.550

Rings
1. Akinori Nakayama, Japan, 19.350
2. Mikhail Voronin, Soviet Union, 19.275
3. Mitsuo Tsukahara, Japan, 19.225
4. Sawao Kato, Japan, 19.150
5. Eizo Kenmotsu, Japan, 18.950

Women

Combined Exercises
1. Ludmila Tourischeva, Soviet Union, 77.025
2. Karin Janz, East Germany, 76.875
3. Tamara Lazakovitch, Soviet Union, 76.850
4. Erika Zuchold, East Germany, 76.450
5. Ljubov Burda, Soviet Union, 75.775

Other placings:
10. Cathy Rigby, US, 74.925
21. Joan Moore, US, 73.450
28. Kimberly Chace, US, 72.925
33. Roxanne Pierce, US, 72.475
36. Linda Metheny, US, 36.250

Team Event
1. Soviet Union, 380.50
2. East Germany, 376.55
3. Hungary, 368.25
4. United States, 365.90
5. Czechoslovakia, 365.00
6. Romania, 360.70
7. Japan, 359.75
8. West Germany, 357.95

Other placings:
18. Britain, 333.95

Vault
1. Karin Janz, East Germany, 19.525
2. Erika Zuchold, East Germany, 19.275
3. Ludmila Tourischeva, Soviet Union, 19.250
4. Ljubov Burda, Soviet Union, 19.225
5. Olga Korbut, Soviet Union, 19.175

Beam
1. Olga Korbut, Soviet Union, 19.400
2. Tamara Lazakovitch, Soviet Union, 19.375
3. Karin Janz, East Germany, 18.975
4. Monika Csaszar, Hungary, 18.925
5. Ludmila Tourischeva, Soviet Union, 18.800

Floor Exercises
1. Olga Korbut, Soviet Union, 19.575
2. Ludmila Tourischeva, Soviet Union, 19.550
3. Tamara Lazakovitch, Soviet Union, 19.450
4. Karin Janz, East Germany, 19.400
5. equal: Ljubov Burda, Soviet Union, 19.100
             Angelika Hellmann, East Germany, 19.100

Asymmetric Bars
1. Karin Janz, East Germany, 19.675
2. equal: Olga Korbut, Soviet Union, 19.450
             Erika Zuchold, East Germany, 19.450

4. Ludmila Tourischeva, Soviet Union, 19.425
5. Ilona Bekesi, Hungary, 19.275

1973 European Championships

Grenoble, France

Men

Combined Exercises
1. Viktor Klimenko, Soviet Union, 56.55
2. Nikolai Andrianov, Soviet Union, 56.30
3. Klaus Koste, East Germany, 55.70

Floor Exercises
1. Nikolai Andrianov, Soviet Union, 18.85
2. Viktor Klimenko, Soviet Union, 18.80
3. Klaus Koste, East Germany, 18.45

High Bar
1. equal: Eberhard Gienger, West Germany, 19.25
   Klaus Koste, East Germany, 19.25
3. Wolfgang Thune, East Germany, 19.20

Parallel Bars
1. Viktor Klimenko, Soviet Union, 18.95
2. equal: Nikolai Andrianov, Soviet Union, 18.75
   Mauno Nissen, Finland, 18.75

Pommel Horse
1. Zoltan Magyar, Hungary, 19.05
2. Wilhelm Kubica, Poland, 18.80
3. Viktor Klimenko, Soviet Union, 18.75

Vault
1. Nikolai Andrianov, Soviet Union, 18.70
2. Andrzej Szajna, Poland, 18.65
3. Imre Molnar, Hungary, 18.15

Rings
1. Viktor Klimenko, Soviet Union, 18.80
2. equal: Nikolai Andrianov, Soviet Union, 18.75
   Daniel Grecu, Romania, 18.75

London, England

Women

Combined Exercises
1. Ludmila Tourischeva, Soviet Union, 38.10
2. Olga Korbut, Soviet Union, 37.65
3. Kerstine Gerschau, East Germany, 37.40

Vault
1. equal: Ludmila Tourischeva, Soviet Union, 18.85
   Angelika Hellmann, East Germany, 18.85
3. Ute Schorn, West Germany, 18.70

Beam
1. Ludmila Tourischeva, Soviet Union, 19.10
2. Alina Goreac, Romania, 18.85
3. Anca Grigoras, Romania, 18.75

Floor Exercises
1. Ludmila Tourischeva, Soviet Union, 18.90
2. Kerstine Gerschau, East Germany, 18.80
3. Alina Goreac, Romania, 18.75

Asymmetric Bars
1. Ludmila Tourischeva, Soviet Union, 19.30
2. Angelika Hellmann, East Germany, 19.25
3. Alina Goreac, Romania, 18.95

1974 World Championships, Varna, Bulgaria

Men

Combined Exercises
1. Shigeru Kasamatsu, Japan, 115.500
2. Nikolai Andrianov, Soviet Union, 115.475
3. Eizo Kenmotsu, Japan, 114.750
4. Hiroshi Kajiyama, Japan, 114.650
5. Mitsuo Tsukahara, Japan, 114.600
Other placings:
25. Wayne Young, US, 110.625
26. Steve Hug, US, 110.550

Team Event
1. Japan, 571.40
2. Soviet Union, 567.35
3. East Germany, 562.40
4. Hungary, 552.80
5. West Germany, 552.65
6. Romania, 547.25
7. Switzerland, 547.20
8. United States, 547.10
Other placings:
15. Britain, 507.35

Floor Exercises
1. Shigeru Kasamatsu, Japan, 19.375
2. Hiroshi Kajiyama, Japan, 19.325
3. Andrei Keranov, Bulgaria, 19.225
4. Vladimir Marchenko, Soviet Union, 19.150
5. Rainer Hanschke, East Germany, 18.900

High Bar
1. Eberhard Gienger, West Germany, 19.500
2. Wolfgang Thune, East Germany, 19.450
3. equal: Eizo Kenmotsu, Japan, 19.275
          Andrzej Szajna, Poland, 19.275
5. Bernd Jager, East Germany, 19.250

Parallel Bars
1. Eizo Kenmotsu, Japan, 19.375
2. Nikolai Andrianov, Soviet Union, 19.325
3. Vladimir Marchenko, Soviet Union, 18.850
4. Hiroshi Kajiyama, Japan, 18.275
5. Bernd Jager, East Germany, 18.100

Pommel Horse
1. Zoltan Magyar, Hungary, 19.575
2. Nikolai Andrianov, Soviet Union, 19.375
3. Eizo Kenmotsu, Japan, 19.225
4. Shigeru Kasamatsu, Japan, 18.950
5. Imre Molnar, Hungary, 18.875

Vault
1. Shigeru Kasamatsu, Japan, 19.325
2. Nikolai Andrianov, Soviet Union, 19.250
3. Hiroshi Kajiyama, Japan, 19.225
4. Andrzej Szajan, Poland, 19.175
5. Eizo Kenmotsu, Japan, 19.075

Rings
1. equal: Nikolai Andrianov, Soviet Union, 19.525
          Dan Grecu, Romania, 19.525
3. Andrzej Szajna, Poland, 19.225
4. Mitsuo Tsukahara, Japan, 19.125
5. Mihai Bors, Romania, 19.000

Women

Combined Exercises
1. Ludmila Tourischeva, Soviet Union, 78.450
2. Olga Korbut, Soviet Union, 77.650
3. Angelika Hellmann, East Germany, 76.875
4. Elvira Saadi, Soviet Union, 76.425
5. Rusadan Siharulidze, Soviet Union, 76.400

Other placings:
18. Joan Rice, US, 74.225
26. Diane Dunbar, US, 73.450
35. Janette Anderson, US, 71.500

Team Event
1. Soviet Union, 384.15
2. East Germany, 376.55
3. Hungary, 370.60
4. Romania, 369.30
5. Czechoslovakia, 368.45
6. Japan, 362.90
7. United States, 362.50
8. West Germany, 361.00

Other placings:
19. Britain, 337.95

Vault
1. Olga Korbut, Soviet Union, 19.450
2. Ludmila Tourischeva, Soviet Union, 19.200
3. Bozena Perdykulova, Czechoslovakia, 19.075
4. Alina Goreac, Romania, 19.025
5. Angelika Hellmann, East Germany, 18.850

Beam
1. Ludmila Tourischeva, Soviet Union, 19.275
2. Olga Korbut, Soviet Union, 19.250
3. Nelli Kim, Soviet Union, 19.200
4. Nina Dronova, Soviet Union, 19.100
5. Alina Goreac, Romania, 18.905

Floor Exercises
1. Ludmila Tourischeva, Soviet Union, 19.775
2. Olga Korbut, Soviet Union, 19.600
3. equal: Rusudan Siharulidze, Soviet Union, 19.550
          Elvira Saadi, Soviet Union, 19.550
5. Nina Dronova, Soviet Union, 19.275

Asymmetric Bars
1. Annelore Zinke, East Germany, 19.650
2. Olga Korbut, Soviet Union, 19.575
3. Ludmila Tourischeva, Soviet Union, 19.500
4. Angelika Hellmann, East Germany, 19.350
5. Richarda Schmeisser, East Germany, 19.250

1975 European Championships

Berne, Switzerland

Men

Combined Exercises
1. Nikolai Andrianov, Soviet Union, 57.90
2. Eberhard Gienger, West Germany, 56.85
3. Alexandr Ditiatin, Soviet Union, 56.70

Floor Exercises
1. equal: Nikolai Andrianov, Soviet Union 19.15
   Andrzej Szajna, Poland, 19.10
3. Jiri Tabak Czechoslovakia, 19.05

High Bar
1. equal: Nikolai Andrianov, Soviet Union, 19.50
   Eberhard Gienger, West Germany, 19.50
3. Andrzej Szajna, Poland, 19.10

Parallel Bars
1. Nikolai Andrianov, Soviet Union, 19.40
2. Alexandr Ditiatin, Soviet Union, 18.95
3. Viktor Klimenko, Soviet Union, 18.75

Pommel Horse
1. Zoltan Magyar, Hungary, 19.50
2. Nikolai Andrianov, Soviet Union, 19.40
3. Eberhard Gienger, West Germany, 19.05

Vault
1. Nikolai Andrianov, Soviet Union, 19.025
2. Alexandr Ditiatin, Soviet Union, 18.975
3. Jiri Tabak, Czechoslovakia, 18.775

Rings
1. Dan Grecu, Romania, 19.60
2. Mihai Bors, Romania, 19.30
3. Alexandr Ditiatin, Soviet Union, 19.15

Skien, Norway

Women

Combined Exercises
1. Nadia Comaneci, Romania, 38.85
2. Nelli Kim, Soviet Union, 38.50
3. Annelore Zinke, East Germany, 37.95

Vault
1. Nadia Comaneci, Romania, 19.50
2. Richarda Schmeisser, East Germany, 19.10
3. equal: Alina Goreac, Romania, 19.00
   Nelli Kim, Soviet Union, 19.00

Beam
1. Nadia Comaneci, Romania, 19.50
2. Nelli Kim, Soviet Union, 19.15
3. Alina Goreac, Romania, 19.00

Floor Exercises
1. Nelli Kim, Soviet Union, 19.55
2. Nadia Comaneci, Romania, 19.40
3. Ludmila Tourischeva, Soviet Union, 19.35

Asymmetric Bars
1. Nadia Comaneci, Romania, 19.65
2. Annelore Zinke, East Germany, 19.55
3. Nelli Kim, Soviet Union, 19.50

1976 Olympics, Montreal, Canada

Men

Combined Exercises
1. Nikolai Andrianov, Soviet Union, 116.650
2. Sawao Kato, Japan, 115.650
3. Mitsuo Tsukahara, Japan, 115.575
4. Alexandr Ditiatin, Soviet Union, 115.525
5. Hiroshi Kajiyama, Japan, 115.425
Other placings :
12. Wayne Young, US, 113.025
15. Peter Kormann, US, 112.475
21. Kurt Thomas, US, 111.175

Team Event
1. Japan, 576.85
2. Soviet Union, 576.45
3. East Germany, 564.65
4. Hungary, 564.45
5. West Germany, 557.40
6. Romania, 557.30
7. United States, 556.10
8. Switzerland, 550.60

Floor Exercises
1. Nikolai Andrianov, Soviet Union, 19.450
2. Vladimir Marchenko, Soviet Union, 19.425
3. Peter Kormann, US, 19.300
4. Roland Bruckner, East Germany, 19.275
5. Sawao Kato, Japan, 19.250

High Bar
1. Mitsuo Tsukahara, Japan, 19.675
2. Eizo Kenmotsu, Japan, 19.500
3. equal: Eberhard Gienger, West Germany, 19.475
   Henri Boerio, France, 19.475
5. Gennadi Kryssin, Soviet Union, 19.250

Parallel Bars
1. Sawao Kato, Japan, 19.675
2. Nikolai Andrianov, Soviet Union, 19.500
3. Mitsuo Tsukahara, Japan, 19.475
4. Bernd Jager, East Germany, 19.200
5. Miloslav Netusil, Czechoslovakia, 19.125

Pommel Horse
1. Zoltan Magyar, Hungary, 19.700
2. Eizo Kenmotsu, Japan, 19.575
3. equal: Nikolai Andrianov, Soviet Union, 19.525
    Michael Nikolay, East Germany, 19.525
5. Sawao Kato, Japan, 19.400

Vault
1. Nikolai Andrianov, Soviet Union, 19.450
2. Mitsuo Tsukahara, Japan, 19.375
3. Hiroshi Kajiyama, Japan, 19.275
4. Dan Grecu, Romania, 19.200
5. equal: Zoltan Magyar, Hungary, 19.150
    Imre Molnar, Hungary, 19.150

Rings:
1. Nikolai Andrianov, Soviet Union, 19.650
2. Alexandr Ditiatin, Soviet Union, 19.550
3. Dan Grecu, Romania, 19.500
4. Ferenc Donath, Hungary, 19.200
5. Eizo Kenmotsu, Japan, 19.175

Women

Combined Exercises
1. Nadia Comaneci, Romania, 79.275
2. Nelli Kim, Soviet Union, 78.675
3. Ludmila Tourischeva, Soviet Union, 78.625
4. Teodora Ungureanu, Romania, 78.375
5. Olga Korbut, Soviet Union, 78.025
Other placings:
14. Kimberley Chace, US, 75.875
18. equal: Debra Wilcox, US, 75.325
    Leslie Wolfsberger, US, 75:325
35. Avril Lennox, Britain, 73.875

Team Event
1. Soviet Union, 390.35
2. Romania, 387.15
3. East Germany, 385.10
4. Hungary, 380.15
5. Czechoslovakia, 378.25
6. United States, 375.05
7. West Germany, 373.50
8. Japan, 372.10

Vault
1. Nelli Kim, Soviet Union, 19.800
2. equal: Ludmila Tourischeva, Soviet Union, 19.665
    Carola Dombeck, East Germany, 19.665
4. Nadia Comaneci, Romania, 19.625
5. Gitta Escher, East Germany, 19.550

Beam
1. Nadia Comaneci, Romania, 19.950
2. Olga Korbut, Soviet Union, 19.725
3. Teodora Ungureanu, Romania, 19.700
4. Ludmila Tourischeva, Soviet Union, 19.475
5. Angelika Hellmann, East Germany, 19.450

Floor Exercises
1. Nelli Kim, Soviet Union, 19.850
2. Ludmila Tourischeva, Soviet Union, 19.825
3. Nadia Comaneci, Romania, 19.750
4. Anna Pohludkova, Czechoslovakia, 19.575
5. Marion Kische, East Germany, 19.475

Asymmetric Bars
1. Nadia Comaneci, Romania, 20.000
2. Teodora Ungureanu, Romania, 19.800
3. Marta Egervari, Hungary, 19.775
4. Marion Kische, East Germany, 19.750
5. Olga Korbut, Soviet Union, 19.300

1977 European Championships

Vilnius, Soviet Union

Men

Combined Exercises
1. Vladimir Markelov, Soviet Union, 57.80
2. Alexandr Tkachev, Soviet Union, 57.25
3. Vladimir Tikhonov, Soviet Union, 57.00

Floor Exercises
1. Alexandr Tkachev, Soviet Union, 19.30
2. Vladimir Markelov, Soviet Union, 19.15
3. Vladimir Tikhonov, Soviet Union, 19.10

High Bar
1. Stojan Deltchev, Bulgaria, 19.35
2. equal: Vladimir Markelov, Soviet Union, 19.25
    Alexandr Tkachev, Soviet Union, 19.25

Parallel Bars
1. Vladimir Tikhonov, Soviet Union, 19.10
2. equal: Ralph Barthel, East Germany, 18.90
   Eberhard Gienger, West Germany, 18.90

Pommel Horse
1. Zoltan Magyar, Hungary, 18.80
2. Michael Nikolay, East Germany, 19.55
3. Vladimir Markelov, Soviet Union, 19.35

Vault
1. equal: Ralph Barthel East Germany, 19.275
   Jiri Tabak, Czechoslovakia, 19.275
3. Vladimir Markelov, Soviet Union, 19.050

Rings
1. Vladimir Markelov, Soviet Union, 19.60
2. Alexandr Tkachev, Soviet Union, 19.40
3. Vladimir Tikhonov, Soviet Union, 19.15

Prague, Czechoslovakia

Women

Combined Exercises
1. Nadia Comaneci, Romania, 39.30
2. Elena Mukhina, Soviet Union, 38.95
3. Nelli Kim, Soviet Union, 38.85

Vault
1. Nelli Kim, Soviet Union, 19.525
2. Nadia Comaneci, Romania, 19.500
3. Elena Mukhina, Soviet Union, 19.450

Beam
1. Elena Mukhina, Soviet Union, 19.40
2. Nelli Kim, Soviet Union, 19.35
3. Maria Filatova, Soviet Union, 19.25

Floor Exercises
1. equal: Maria Filatova, Soviet Union, 19.70
   Elena Mukhina, Soviet Union, 19.70
3. Nelli Kim, Soviet Union, 19.55

Asymmetric Bars
1. equal: Nadia Comaneci, Romania, 19.65
   Elena Mukhina, Soviet Union, 19.65
3. Steffi Kraker, East Germany, 19.60

1978 World Championships, Strasbourg, France

Men

Combined Exercises
1. Nikolai Andrianov, Soviet Union, 117.200
2. Eizo Kenmotsu, Japan, 116.500
3. Alexandr Ditiatin, Soviet Union, 116.375
4. Eberhard Gienger, West Germany, 116.200
5. Hiroji Kajiyama, Japan, 115.900
Other placings :
6. Kurt Thomas, US, 115.725
9. Bart Conner, US, 115.200
20. Mike Wilson, US, 113.800
34. Ian Neale, Britain, 110.600
39. equal: James Hartung, US, 111.600
    Philip Cahoy, US, 111.600
42. Pete Kormann, US, 111.500
83. Tommy Wilson, Britain, 107.050

Team Event
1. Japan, 579.85
2. Soviet Union, 578.95
3. East Germany, 571.75
4. United States, 568.70
5. West Germany, 566.90
6. Hungary, 566.30
7. Romania, 560.85
8. France, 556.35
Other placings :
17. Britain, 536.00

Floor Exercises
1. Kurt Thomas, US, 19.650
2. Shigeru Kasamatsu, Japan, 19.575
3. Alexandr Ditiatin, Soviet Union, 19.400
4. Nikolai Andrianov, Soviet Union, 19.350
5. Stojan Deltchev, Bulgaria, 19.200

High Bar
1. Shigeru Kasamatsu, Japan, 19.675
2. Eberhard Gienger, West Germany, 19.650
3. equal: Stojan Deltchev, Bulgaria, 19.600
   Gennadi Krysin, Soviet Union, 19.600
5. Alexandr Tkachev, Soviet Union, 19.500

Parallel Bars
1. Eizo Kenmotsu, Japan, 19.600
2. equal: Nikolai Andrianov, Soviet Union, 19.575
   Hiroji Kajiyama, Japan, 19.575
4. Alexandr Tkachev, Soviet Union, 19.450
5. Bart Conner, US, 19.375

Pommel Horse
1. Zoltan Magyar, Hungary, 19.800
2. Eberhard Gienger, West Germany, 19.425
3. Stojan Deltchev, Bulgaria, 19.400
4. equal: Alexandr Ditiatin, Soviet Union, 19.350
   Ferenc Donath, Hungary, 19.350

Vault
1. Junichi Shimizu, Japan, 19.600
2. Nikolai Andrianov, Soviet Union, 19.575
3. Ralph Barthel, East Germany, 19.550
4. Alexandr Ditiatin, Soviet Union, 19.475
5. Lutz Mack, East Germany, 19.400

Rings
1. Nikolai Andrianov, Soviet Union, 19.700
2. Alexandr Ditiatin, Soviet Union, 19.675
3. Dan Grecu, Romania, 19.650
4. Shigeru Kasamatsu, Japan, 19.525
5. Lutz Mack, East Germany, 19.500

Women

Combined Exercises
1. Elena Mukhina, Soviet Union, 78.725
2. Nelli Kim, Soviet Union, 78.575
3. Natalia Shaposhnikova, Soviet Union, 77.875
4. Nadia Comaneci, Romania, 77.725
5. Emilia Eberle, Romania, 77.300
Other placings :
8. Kathy Johnson, US, 76.825
9. Rhonda Schwandt, US, 76.650
20. Marica Frederick, US, 75.50
43. Christa Canary, US, 74.00
44. equal: Leslie Pyfer, US, 73.95
46. Donna Turnbow, US, 73.85
67. Susan Cheesebrough, Britain, 72.65
83. Karen Robb, Britain, 71.85
99. Joanna Sime, Britain, 70.95

Team Event
1. Soviet Union, 388.75
2. Romania, 384.25
3. East Germany, 382.25
4. Hungary, 377.80
5. United States, 377.20
6. Czechoslovakia, 376.95
7. Japan, 370.60
8. Canada, 369.90

Other placings :
16. Britain, 358.50

Vault
1. Nelli Kim, Soviet Union, 19.625
2. Nadia Comaneci, Romania, 19.600
3. Steffi Kraker, East Germany, 19.550
4. Rhonda Schwandt, US, 19.525
5. Emilia Eberle, Romania, 19.450

Beam
1. Nadia Comaneci, Romania, 19.625
2. Elena Mukhina, Soviet Union, 19.600
3. Emilia Eberle, Romania, 19.575
4. Eva Ovari, Hungary, 19.400
5. Vera Cerna, Czechoslovakia, 19.300

Floor Exercises
1. equal: Nelli Kim, Soviet Union, 19.775
   Elena Mukhina Soviet Union, 19.775
3. equal: Kathy Johnson, US, 19.525
   Emilia Eberle, Romania, 19.525
5. Silvia Hindorff, East Germany, 19.475

Asymmetric Bars
1. Marcia Frederick, US, 19.800
2. Elena Mukhina, Soviet Union, 19.725
3. Emilia Eberle, Romania, 19.625
4. Maria Filatova, Soviet Union, 19.600
5. Nadia Comaneci, Romania, 19.575

1979 European Championships

Essen, West Germany

Men

Combined Exercises
1. Stojan Deltchev, Bulgaria, 57.75
2. equal: Alexandr Tkachev, Soviet Union, 57.45
   Bogdan Makuz, Soviet Union, 57.45

Floor Exercises
1. Stojan Deltchev, Bulgaria, 19.60
2. Ralph Barthel, East Germany, 19.50
3. Lutz Mack, East Germany, 19.45

High Bar
1. Alexandr Tkachev, Soviet Union, 19.55
2. equal: Stojan Deltchev, Bulgaria, 19.45
   Peter Kovacs, Hungary, 19.45

Parallel Bars
1. Bogdan Makuz, Soviet Union, 19.55
2. Alexandr Ditiatin, Soviet Union, 19.40
3. equal: Henri Boerio, France, 19.30
   Eberhard Gienger, West Germany, 19.30

Pommel Horse
1. equal: Alexandr Ditiatin, Soviet Union, 19.15
   Guczoghy, Hungary, 19.15
3. equal: Michel Boutard, France, 19.05
   Bogdan Makuz, Soviet Union, 19.05

Vault
1. Bogdan Makuz, Soviet Union, 19.500
2. Josef Konecky, Czechoslovakia, 19.475
3. equal: Stojan Deltchev, Bulgaria, 19.400
   Ralph Barthel, East Germany, 19.400

Rings
1. Alexandr Ditiatin, Soviet Union, 19.35
2. Bogdan Makuz, Soviet Union, 19.20
3. Lutz Mack, East Germany, 19.15

Copenhagen, Denmark

Women

Combined Exercises
1. Nadia Comaneci, Romania, 39.45
2. Emilia Eberle, Romania, 38.85
3. Natalia Shaposhnikova, Soviet Union, 38.75

Vault
1. Nadia Comaneci, Romania, 19.775
2. Maxi Gnauck, East Germany, 19.550
3. Natalia Shaposhnikova, Soviet Union, 19.525

Beam
1. Natalia Shaposhnikova, Soviet Union, 19.85
2. Emilia Eberle, Romania, 19.60
3. Nadia Comaneci, Romania, 19.25

Floor Exercises
1. Nadia Comaneci, Romania, 19.60
2. equal: Elena Mukhina, Soviet Union, 19.20
   Natalia Shaposhnikova, Soviet Union, 19.20

Asymmetric Bars
1. Elena Mukhina, Soviet Union, 19.70
2. Emilia Eberle, Romania, 19.65
3. Maxi Gnauck, East Germany, 19.60

1979 World Championships, Fort Worth, Dallas, United States

Men

Combined Exercises
1. Alexandr Ditiatin, Soviet Union, 118.250
2. Kurt Thomas, US, 117.975
3. Alexandr Tkachev, Soviet Union, 117.475
4. Vladimir Markelov, Soviet Union, 117.275
5. Bart Conner, US, 117.025
Other placings :
9. equal: James Hartung, US, 116.450
82. Tommy Wilson, Britain, 110.60
90. Jeff Davis, Britain, 110.20

Team Event
1. Soviet Union, 587.500
2. Japan, 583.700
3. United States, 581.150
4. East Germany, 581.000
5. China, 578.950
6. Hungary, 573.600
7. West Germany, 570.350
8. Romania, 569.750
9. Bulgaria, 567.650
10. Czechoslovakia, 562.350
Other placings :
18. Britain 547.050

Floor Exercises
1. equal: Kurt Thomas, US, 19.800
   Roland Bruckner, East Germany, 19.800
3. Alexandr Tkachev, Soviet Union, 19.775
4. Nikolai Andrianov, Soviet Union, 19.725
5. Bart Conner, US, 19.700

High Bar
1. Kurt Thomas, US, 19.775
2. Alexandr Tkachev, Soviet Union, 19.750
3. Alexandr Ditiatin, Soviet Union, 19.675
4. Stojan Deltchev, Bulgaria, 19.550
5. equal: Fei Tong, China, 19.500
   Michael Nikolay, East Germany, 19.500

Parallel Bars
1. Bart Conner, US, 19.725
2. equal: Kurt Thomas, US, 19.700
   Alexandr Tkachev, Soviet Union, 19.700
4. equal: Koji Gushiken, Japan, 19.600
   Alexandr Ditiatin, Soviet Union, 19.600

Pommel Horse
1. Zoltan Magyar, Hungary, 19.825
2. Kurt Thomas, US, 19.725
3. Koji Gushiken, Japan, 19.600
4. Alexandr Ditiatin, Soviet Union, 19.550
5. Stojan Deltchev, Bulgaria, 19.525

Vault
1. Alexandr Ditiatin, Soviet Union, 19.725
2. Nikolai Andrianov, Soviet Union, 19.700
3. equal: Bart Conner, US, 19.675
   Ralph Barthel, East Germany, 19.675
5. Roland Bruckner, East Germany, 19.600

Rings
1. Alexandr Ditiatin, Soviet Union, 19.800
2. Dan Grecu, Romania, 19.700
3. Alexandr Tkachev, Soviet Union, 19.675
4. Koji Gushiken, Japan, 19.650
5. Stojan Deltchev, Bulgaria, 19.625

Women

Combined Exercises
1. Nelli Kim, Soviet Union, 78.650
2. Maxi Gnauck, East Germany, 78.375
3. Melita Ruhn, Romania, 78.325
4. Maria Filatova, Soviet Union, 77.950
5. Rodica Dunca, Romania, 77.725
Other placings:
12. Leslie Pyfer, US, 76.825
19. Suzy Kellems, US, 75.975
23. Marcia Frederick, US, 75.750
37. Kathy Johnson, US, retired before final
67. Susan Cheesebrough, Britain, 73.850
83. Kathleen Williams, Britain, 73.050
91. Suzanne Dando, Britain, 72.700
92. Mandy Gornall, Britain, 72.650

Team Event
1. Romania, 389.550
2. Soviet Union, 388.925
3. East Germany, 388.075
4. China, 384.600
5. Czechoslovakia, 382.300
6. United States, 381.325
7. Hungary, 379.050
8. Bulgaria, 376.950
Other placings:
16. Britain, 366.600

Vault
1. Dumitrata Turner, Romania, 19.775
2. Stella Zakharova, Soviet Union, 19.700
3. equal: Steffi Kraker, East Germany, 19.675
   Nelli Kim, Soviet Union, 19.675
5. Christa Canary, US, 19.638

Beam
1. Vera Cerna, Czechoslovakia, 19.800
2. Nelli Kim, Soviet Union, 19.625
3. Regina Grabolle, East Germany, 19.575
4. Eva Mareckova, Czechoslovakia, 19.550
5. Maria Filatova, Soviet Union, 19.525

Floor Exercises
1. Emilia Eberle, Romania, 19.800
2. Nelli Kim, Soviet Union, 19.775
3. Melita Ruhn, Romania, 19.725
4. Maxi Gnauck, East Germany, 19.700
5. Maria Filatova, Soviet Union, 19.650

Asymmetric Bars
1. equal: Ma Yan Hong, China, 19.825
   Maxi Gnauck, East Germany, 19.825
3. Emilia Eberle, Romania, 19.750
4. Steffi Kraker, East Germany, 19.700
5. Nelli Kim, Soviet Union, 19.625

1980 Olympics, Moscow, Soviet Union
Men

Combined Exercises
1. Alexandr Ditiatin, Soviet Union, 118.650
2. Nikolai Andrianov, Soviet Union, 118.225
3. Stojan Deltchev, Bulgaria, 118.000
4. Alexandr Tkachev, Soviet Union, 117.700
5. Roland Bruckner, East Germany, 117.300
Other placings:
30. Barry Winch, Britain, 111.125
31. Tommy Wilson, Britain, 110.375
35. Keith Langley, Britain, 109.625

Team Event
1. Soviet Union, 589.60
2. East Germany, 581.15

3. Hungary, 575.00
4. Romania, 572.30
5. Bulgaria, 571.55
6. Czechoslovakia, 569.80
7. Cuba, 563.20
8. France, 559.20

Floor Exercises
1. Roland Bruckner, East Germany, 19.750
2. Nikolai Andrianov, Soviet Union, 19.725
3. Alexandr Ditiatin, Soviet Union, 19.725
4. Jiri Tabak, Czechoslovakia, 19.675
5. Peter Kovacs, Hungary, 19.425

High Bar
1. Stojan Deltchev, Bulgaria, 19.825
2. Alexandr Ditiatin, Soviet Union, 19.750
3. Nikolai Andrianov, Soviet Union, 19.675
4. Ralf-Peter Hemman, East Germany, 19.525
5. Michael Nikolay, East Germany, 19.525

Parallel Bars
1. Alexandr Tkachev, Soviet Union, 19.775
2. Alexandr Ditiatin, Soviet Union, 19.750
3. Roland Bruckner, East Germany, 19.650
4. Michael Nikolay, East Germany, 19.600
5. Stojan Deltchev, Bulgaria, 19.575

Pommel Horse
1. Zoltan Magyar, Hungary, 19.925
2. Alexandr Ditiatin, Soviet Union, 19.800
3. Michael Nikolay, East Germany, 19.775
4. Roland Bruckner, East Germany, 19.725
5. Alexandr Tkachev, Soviet Union, 19.475

Vault
1. Nikolai Andrianov, Soviet Union, 19.825
2. Alexandr Ditiatin, Soviet Union, 19.800
3. Roland Bruckner, East Germany, 19.775
4. Ralf-Peter Hemman, East Germany, 19.750
5. Stojan Deltchev, Bulgaria, 19.700

Rings
1. Alexandr Ditiatin, Soviet Union, 19.875
2. Alexandr Tkachev, Soviet Union, 19.725
3. Jiri Tabak, Czechoslovakia, 19.600
4. Roland Bruckner, East Germany, 19.575
5. Stojan Deltchev, Bulgaria, 19.475

Women

Combined Exercises
1. Elena Davydova, Soviet Union, 79.150

2. equal: Maxi Gnauck, East Germany, 79.075
   Nadia Comaneci, Romania, 79.075
4. Natalia Shaposhnikova, Soviet Union, 79.025
5. Nelli Kim, Soviet Union, 78.425

Other placings :
23. Denise Jones, Britain, 72.375
27. Suzanne Dando, Britain, 70.775
28. Susan Cheesebrough, Britain, 70.725

Team Event
1. Soviet Union, 394.90
2. Romania, 393.50
3. East Germany, 392.55
4. Czechoslovakia, 388.80
5. Hungary, 384.30
6. Bulgaria, 382.10
7. Poland, 376.25
8. North Korea, 364.05

Vault
1. Natalia Shaposhnikova, Soviet Union, 19.725
2. Steffi Kraker, East Germany, 19.675
3. Melita Ruhn, Romania, 19.650
4. Elena Davydova, Soviet Union, 19.575
5. Nadia Comaneci, Romania, 19.350

Beam
1. Nadia Comaneci, Romania, 19.800
2. Elena Davydova, Soviet Union, 19.750
3. Natalia Shaposhnikova, Soviet Union, 19.725
4. Maxi Gnauck, East Germany, 19.700
5. Radka Zemanova, Czechoslovakia, 19.650

Floor Exercises
1. equal: Nelli Kim, Soviet Union, 19.875
   Nadia Comaneci, Romania, 19.875
3. equal: Natalia Shaposhnikova, Soviet Union, 19.825
   Maxi Gnauck, East Germany, 19.825
5. Emilia Eberle, Romania, 19.750

Asymmetric Bars
1. Maxi Gnauck, East Germany, 19.875
2. Emilia Eberle, Romania, 19.850
3. equal: Steffi Kraker, East Germany, 19.775
   Melita Ruhn, Romania, 19.775
   Maria Filatova, Soviet Union, 19.775

1981 European Championships

Rome, Italy

Men

Combined Exercises
1. Alexandr Tkachev, Soviet Union, 58.60
2. Yuri Korolev, Soviet Union, 58.30
3. Bogdan Makuz, Soviet Union, 58.20

Floor Exercises
1. equal: Yuri Korolev, Soviet Union, 19.65
   Roland Bruckner, East Germany, 19.65
3. Alexandr Tkachev, Soviet Union, 19.55

High Bar
1. equal: Alexandr Tkachev, Soviet Union, 19.80
   Eberhard Gienger, West Germany, 19.80
3. Bogdan Makuz, Soviet Union, 19.60

Parallel Bars
1. Bogdan Makuz, Soviet Union, 19.70
2. Alexandr Tkachev, Soviet Union, 19.45
3. Lutz Hoffmann, East Germany, 19.40

Pommel Horse
1. Gyorgy Guczoghy, Hungary, 19.75
2. equal: Michel Boutard, France, 19.55
   Kurt Szilier, Romania, 19.55
   Yuri Korolev, Soviet Union, 19.55

Vault
1. Bogdan Makuz, Soviet Union, 19.60
2. Yuri Korolev, Soviet Union, 19.57
3. Rocco Amboni, Italy, 19.50

Rings
1. Yuri Korolev, Soviet Union, 19.80
2. Rocco Amboni, Italy, 19.65
3. Alexandr Tkachev, Soviet Union, 19.60

Madrid, Spain

Women

Combined Exercises
1. Maxi Gnauck, East Germany, 39.25
2. Christina Grigoras, Romania, 38.95
3. Alla Misnik, Soviet Union, 38.80

Vault
1. Christina Grigoras, Romania, 19.60
2. equal: Maxi Gnauck, East Germany, 19.55
   Birgit Senff, East Germany, 19.55

Beam
1. Maxi Gnauck, East Germany, 19.35
2. Natalia Ilenko, Soviet Union, 19.25
3. Rodica Dunca, Romania, 19.15

Floor Exercises
1. Maxi Gnauck, East Germany, 19.65
2. Alla Misnik, Soviet Union, 19.45
3. Christina Grigoras, Romania, 19.25

Asymmetric Bars
1. Maxi Gnauck, East Germany, 19.95
2. equal: Christina Grigoras, Romania, 19.60
   Alla Misnik, Soviet Union, 19.60

1981 World Championships, Moscow, Soviet Union

Men

Combined Exercises
1. Yuri Korolev, Soviet Union, 118.375
2. Bogdan Makuz, Soviet Union, 118.350
3. Koji Gushiken, Japan, 117.975
4. Fei Tong, China, 117.700
5. Roland Bruckner, East Germany, 117.325

Other placings:
11. Bart Conner, US, 116.750
13. Peter Vidmar, US, 116.450
15. Jim Hartung, US, 115.925
42. Scott Johnson, US, 114.15
45. Philip Cahoy, US, 113.95
67. Keith Langley, Britain, 112.20
70. Tim Daggett, US, 112.15
92. Barry Winch, Britain, 110.50
96. Andrew Morris, Britain, 109.90

Team Event
1. Soviet Union, 588.95
2. Japan, 585.85
3. China, 583.90
4. East Germany, 583.75
5. United States, 577.30
6. West Germany, 576.10
7. France, 573.25
8. Hungary, 572.55
9. Romania, 570.60
10. Bulgaria, 569.80

Other placing:
17. Britain 552.25

Floor Exercises
1. equal: Yuri Korolev, Soviet Union, 19.775
   Li Yuejiu, China, 19.775

3. Koji Gushiken, Japan, 19.650
4. Peng Yanping, China, 19.475
5. Alexandr Tkachev, Soviet Union, 19.450

High Bar
1. Alexandr Tkachev, Soviet Union, 19.900
2. equal: Eberhard Gienger, West Germany, 19.875
   Artur Agopian, Soviet Union, 19.875
4. Kiyoshi Goto, Japan, 19.825
5. Li Ning, China, 19.750

Parallel Bars
1. equal: Alexandr Ditiatin, Soviet Union, 19.825
   Koji Gushiken, Japan, 19.825
3. Nobuyuki Kajitani, Japan, 19.800
4. Bogdan Makuz, Soviet Union, 19.775
5. Michael Nikolay, East Germany, 19.725

Pommel Horse
1. equal: Michael Nikolay, East Germany, 19.900
   Li Xiaoping, China, 19.900
3. equal: Yuri Korolev, Soviet Union, 19.875
   Gyorgy Guczoghy, Hungary, 19.875
5. Kiyoshi Goto, Japan, 19.750

Vault
1. Ralf-Peter Hemman, East Germany, 19.900
2. Artur Agopian, Soviet Union, 19.850
3. Bogdan Makuz, Soviet Union, 19.800
4. Casimiro Suarez, Cuba, 19.750
5. Michael Nikolay, East Germany, 19.650

Rings
1. Alexandr Ditiatin, Soviet Union, 19.825
2. Huang Yubin, China, 19.700
3. Bogdan Makuz, Soviet Union, 19.650
4. Tong Fei, China, 19.625
5. Nobuyuki Kajitani, Japan, 19.600

Women

Combined Exercises
1. Olga Bitcherova, Soviet Union, 78.400
2. Maria Filatova, Soviet Union, 78.075
3. Elena Davydova, Soviet Union, 77.925
4. Ma Yan Hong, China, 77.625
5. Christina Grigoras, Romania, 77.125

Other placings :
7. Julianne McNamara, US, 76.900
14. Kathy Johnson, US, 76.400
20. Tracee Talavera, US, 76.175

25. Amy Koopman, US, 75.50
35. Mandy Gornall, Britain, 72.675
    (achieved in final)
35. Michelle Goodwin, US, 74.80
    (achieved in team competition)
40. Gina Stallone, US, 74.55
71. Hayley Price, Britain, 71.55
75. Kathy Williams, Britain, 71.25
76. Cheryl Weatherstone, Britain, 71.20
85. Lisa Young, Britain, 70.60
93. Denise Jones, Britain, 69.20

Team Event
1. Soviet Union, 389.30
2. China, 384.60
3. East Germany, 382.10
4. Romania, 381.50
5. Czechoslovakia, 379.65
6. United States, 379.45
7. Bulgaria, 377.90
8. Hungary, 372.30
9. West Germany, 371.30
10. Canada, 366.80

Other placing :
12. Britain 359.40

Vault
1. Maxi Gnauck, East Germany, 19.675
2. Stella Zakharova, Soviet Union, 19.500
3. Steffi Kraker, East Germany, 19.475
4. Elena Davydova, Soviet Union, 19.325
5. Lavinia Agache, Romania, 19.275

Beam
1. Maxi Gnauck, East Germany, 19.525
2. Chen Yong Yang China, 19.275
3. equal: Tracee Talavera, US, 19.250
   Wu Jiani, China, 19.250
5. Julianne McNamara, US, 19.225

Floor Exercises
1. Natalia Ilenko, Soviet Union, 19.850
2. Elena Davydova, Soviet Union, 19.775
3. Zoya Grancharova, Bulgaria, 19.675
4. Wu Jiani, China, 19.525
5. equal: Ma Yan Hong, China, 19.450
   Rodica Dunca, Romania, 19.450

Asymmetric Bars
1. Maxi Gnauck, East Germany, 19.900
2. Ma Yan Hong, China, 19.800
3. equal: Julianne McNamara, US, 19.700
   Elena Davydova, Soviet Union, 19.700
5. Christina Grigoras, Romania, 19.650

Index

PHOTOGRAPH ACKNOWLEDGEMENTS

Black and white : frontispiece, Colorsport; page 10, Mary Evans Picture Library; page 13, Keystone Press; page 14 top, Bavaria-Verlag Bildagentur; page 14 bottom, Pressens Bild; page 15, Mary Evans Picture Library; page 21 top, BBC Hulton Picture Library; page 21 bottom, Press Association; page 23, Central Press; page 24, Central Press; page 25, Central Press; page 26, Keystone Press; page 27, Keystone Press; page 28, Keystone Press; page 29, Novosti Press Agency; page 31, Alan Burrows; page 32 top, Novosti Press Agency; page 32 bottom, Alan Burrows; page 33, Fox Photos Ltd; page 34, Alan Burrows; page 35, Central Press; page 36, Novosti Press Agency; page 37 top, Novosti Press Agency; page 37 bottom, Alan Burrows; page 39, Popperfoto; page 40, Popperfoto; page 41, Alan Burrows; page 43 top, Popperfoto; page 43 bottom, Popperfoto; page 44, Alan Burrows; page 45, Alan Burrows; page 46, Alan Burrows; page 47, Novosti Press Agency; page 48, Novosti Press Agency; page 49, Novosti Press Agency; page 51, Colorsport; page 52, All-Sport; page 53, Popperfoto; page 54, All-Sport; page 56, All-Sport; page 58, All-Sport; page 60, Novosti Press Agency; page 61, All-Sport; page 62, Popperfoto; page 63 top, Colorsport; page 63 bottom, Novosti Press Agency; page 64, Novosti Press Agency; page 65, Alan Burrows; page 68, Alan Burrows; page 70, All-Sport; page 71 top, Popperfoto; page 71 bottom, Popperfoto; page 72, All-Sport; page 73, Novosti Press Agency; page 74, Novosti Press Agency; page 75, Colorsport; page 76, Colorsport; page 77, Keystone Press Agency; page 79, Novosti Press Agency; page 80 left, Colorsport; page 80 right, Colorsport; page 81 left, All-Sport; page 81 right, Rich Kenney; page 83, Colorsport; page 84, Colorsport; page 85, All-Sport; page 86 left, Novosti Press Agency; page 86 right, Colorsport; page 88, All-Sport; page 89 top, Colorsport; page 89 bottom, Colorsport; page 90, Colorsport; page 91, Colorsport; page 92, All-Sport; page 93, Colorsport; page 94, Colorsport; page 95, All-Sport; page 96, Colorsport; page 97 left, Colorsport; page 97 right, All-Sport; page 98, All-Sport; page 99, All-Sport; page 101, All-Sport

Colour : Olga Korbut, Vera Caslavska, Mitsuo Tsukahara, Ludmila Tourischeva, Eizo Kenmotsu, Cathy Rigby, Nadia Comaneci, Nelli Kim, Natalia Shaposhnikova by All-Sport; Alexandr Ditiatin and Elena Davydova by Colorsport